Don't Be Afraid of Change
(Spare Change, That Is!)

This book is for anyone who has ever worried about how to pay the bills, felt guilty buying something for themselves, or used the phrase, "I can't afford it."

There is another way to think and feel about your finances and your ability to create wealth in your life. Money is actually just energy, and the energy of the Universe is an unlimited resource from which we can draw physical and spiritual abundance. The key to prosperous living lies in your willingness to take back your own power to manifest change. *Silver's Spells for Prosperity* reminds you that you already have the power to change things, and gives you a delightful bag of tricks for banishing poverty and opening the door to personal abundance!

To Write to the Author

If you wish to contact the author or would like more information about this book, please write to:

Silver RavenWolf
℅ Llewellyn Worldwide
P.O. Box 64383, Dept. K726-9
St. Paul, MN 55164-0383, U.S.A.

or visit Silver's web site at
http://www.silverravenwolf.com

Please enclose a self-addressed stamped envelope for reply, or $1.00 to cover costs. If outside U.S.A., enclose international postal reply coupon.

Silver's Spells for

PROSPERITY

Silver RavenWolf

2000
Llewellyn Publications
St. Paul, Minnesota 55164-0383

FIRST EDITION
Second Printing, 2000

Cover art by Bill Cannon
Cover design by Anne Marie Garrison
Editing and book design by Rebecca Zins
Illustrations by Shelly Bartek (except pages 21 and 161 by Llewellyn Art Department)

Library of Congress Cataloging-in-Publication Data
RavenWolf, Silver, 1956–
    Silver's spells for prosperity / Silver RavenWolf. —1st ed.
        p.   cm.
    Includes bibliographical references (p.   ) and index.
    ISBN 1-56718-726-9 (trade paper)
    1. Magic.   2. Finance, Personal—Miscellanea.   I. Title.
BF1623.F55R38   1999
133.4'4—dc21   99-17322
                                                              CIP

Llewellyn Worldwide does not participate in, endorse, or have any authority
or responsibility concerning private business transactions between our authors
and the public.
    All mail addressed to the author is forwarded but the publisher cannot, unless
specifically instructed by the author, give out an address or phone number.

Disclaimer: These spells are not to be used in lieu of professional advice.

Llewellyn Publications
A Division of Llewellyn Worldwide, Ltd.
P.O. Box 64383, Dept. K726-9
St. Paul, MN 55164-0383, U.S.A.

Printed in the United States of America on recycled paper

Other Books by Silver RavenWolf

In the *Silver's Spells* Series

This book is dedicated to:

Those folks who are so broke
they have to dig in the couch
cushions for errant quarters

Contents

Bills . . . Magickal Tips When Writing Checks
or Money Orders . . . When You Mail Your
Bills . . . Relieving the Debt Monster's Emo-
tional Pressure . . . Don't Spend Today—
Breathe Easier Tomorrow . . . Do I Really
Need It? . . . Spell to Curb Frivolous Spending
. . . Banishing the Financial Fog . . . Magickal
Receipt Envelope . . . Beating the Credit Card
Scam . . . The Ten-Dollar Spell . . . Banishing
Blocks to your Financial Success with the
Elements . . . Banishing Blocks with Earth
Gnomes . . . Banishing Blocks with Air
Sylphs . . . Banishing Blocks with Fire Sala-
manders . . . Banishing Blocks with Water
Undines . . . Collecting Debts . . . You Owe
Me Spell . . . To Get a Creditor Off Your Back
. . . Don't Give Up . . . Quickies for Banishing
. . . General Emergencies

About Silver . . .

"The best way for a magickal person to be accepted is to let people get to know you," explains Silver. "Once they understand your personal values and principles, their attitudes about your alternative religion interests tend to be more positive. Let them know you for the work that you do." Silver extensively tours the United States, giving seminars and lectures about magickal religions and practices, and estimates that she has met over 15,000 magickal individuals in the last four years. Silver is the Clan Head of the Black Forest Family that includes eleven covens in eight states.

Silver has spent the last fifteen years of her life developing and implementing spiritually focused courses to assist in enhancing the individual lifestyle in a practical way. *Silver's Spells for Prosperity* is an encapsulation of one of her training courses.

1

On your mark!
Get set!

Come join the fun! I've got all sorts of things in here for you. There are ideas on how to allow yourself to enjoy prosperity, how to banish those awful old debts without heartache, how to get money back from someone who owes you, how to transform your money flow in a positive way, and much more. I also provide historical and practical information on spell elements and ingredients. It's fun to learn and zap, too!

1

Welcome to my world—a universe of abundance where prosperity is what you bring to your work, not what your work brings to you.

The spells in this book represent my journey from poverty to abundance in a practical and magickal way. No kidding! Right now you are holding the very plan I used to create prosperity in my life.

I know you are just itching to get to the spells, but please take a moment to peruse this little chapter, 'cuz there's stuff in here that will make or break your spellcasting finesse. I'll keep this short—I promise!

The first step to living a prosperous life lies in your desire to exercise your right to take back your power. By *acknowledging* that you have the power to change things while you are having fun, you open the door to your personal prosperity. Truly, prosperity means having the time of your life.

Prosperity magick[1] deals with your state of mind. In prosperity magick, if you think yourself poor, you *will* be

----

1. Magick spelled with a "k" denotes real magick—using your will to create form—as opposed to the illusionary magic used by many fine entertainers.

poor. This is the same in love and healing magick but, for some reason, many people just can't believe that how they *think* manifests into hard financial dollars and cents. When I started looking at money and seeing energy rather than printed paper or embossed metal, I realized a shocking and simple truth: money is just energy. The mystery of money immediately vanished!

You are already a prosperous person. You just have to acknowledge that fact!

Balance

All workings of magick and ritual create energies to push or pull life into balance. Recently one of my students, let's call her Heather, buried herself in an onslaught of prosperity magick. As she was just about to reach her goal, she said, "I think it's wonderful that the Goddess changes everything She touches, but I wish She would leave Her hands off for awhile, at least until I gain some equilibrium!" Then Heather laughed, and said, "I didn't realize my life was so out of whack, but boy, has this been worth it!" One week later, she finished closing on the house she'd always wanted. How long did it take Heather to manifest her goal, from beginning to end? Six weeks. Of course, gaining a home is only one aspect of Heather's prosperity work (albeit a large one). She had other, smaller successes along the way—and some startling realizations about herself, her mission in life, and how she fit into the general nature of things. The house was only a material benefit.

Does this mean that scary things are going to happen? No. It just means that once you begin to seriously work prosperity magick, things will be different!

Correspondences

Most magickal applications contain correspondences. Correspondences are items or energies that relate to the focus of the issue. In this book, our focus is on prosperity. Throughout the book I've provided various correspondences for each spell. I've also given you a few lists in the appendices to aid you in substitutions as you learn to write your own spells.

Correspondences include: planetary hours, deities, herbs, oils, planets, totem animals, magickal alphabets, phases of the moon, colors, and elements. Remember, you don't have to use all the correspondences I mention in any spell. If you're not into angels, then don't use those listed. If you don't particularly like to use plant energies, then don't use them. Substitutions are acceptable. I am simply presenting you with the wide range of choices that have worked for me.

Timing

How long will it take your spell to manifest?

- Small goals normally (but not always) manifest faster than large goals, usually within thirty days (or moon to moon).

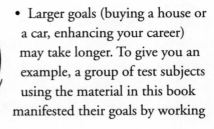

- Larger goals (buying a house or a car, enhancing your career) may take longer. To give you an example, a group of test subjects using the material in this book manifested their goals by working

several spells spaced over time (this is called "building")
and reaped the following benefits:

Angela—house—6 weeks
George—house—4 weeks
Sheila—house—6 months
Linda—published her book—3 months
Pat—job promotion—2 months
Harry—curbed spending habits—5 months

- The old teachers said, "Do a spell, then forget it." These
teachers meant: do the spell, but don't worry about it.
Feeding negative thoughts into your spellwork will
defeat your purpose. If you worry about the manifestation of the spell, then you create blocks in the path of
that manifestation, and it will take longer to make
things happen. Magick follows the path of least resistance so, unless you have a reason for guiding the magick
along a particular line of thought, just let the magick go.

- Don't try to direct your spell too much. Let's say you
need money, but you've tried every way possible in the
regular world with no success. Now you want to do

magick. If you think that the only way money will come to you is through the means you have already tried, you will fail. Leave the path to money up to Spirit, or Divinity. You should still keep working in the "real world" to help manifest your desires, too.

- Keep in mind that your own creativity and needs carry important weight in spellcasting. If today is Sunday and the spell calls for completion on a Monday, but you really need to do the spell today, then go ahead and do the spell today. If the spell calls for a supply that you don't have, that's okay. Substitute something else.

Learning to Devise a Spiritual Plan

Throwing magick at a problem or goal isn't the ultimate answer to our problems. Magickal people think carefully before choosing a magickal technique or spell. You need to consider an entire plan of action, of which magick becomes a part. Yes, a spell can take only a few minutes to do, and a prayer a moment or two to utter, but without a complete spiritual plan, you may be throwing snowflakes at a campfire.

A complete spiritual plan includes:

- Logical thought about the goal or situation.

- Considering how your actions, both magickal and mundane, will affect the outcome of the goal, situation, or other people.

- Building positive reinforcement around you.

- Reprogramming your mind to accept success through thought, word, and action.

- Involving Divinity as much as possible in what you do.

I know all this seems a little complicated for something like a simple spell, but if we learn to plan wisely, we have a better chance for success. Many of the spells in this book can be linked together to help you design a spiritual plan.

Why Magick Doesn't Always Work

Every adept magickal individual has experienced (shudder!) failure. Through failure we learn and grow. Don't think because you happily zap away that all will turn out the way you want it to. Remember, *magick follows the path of least resistance,* and if we are not careful and are not specific with our requests, failure may come as a result.

Sometimes Spirit knows better than we do what will be right for us. I've always taught my students (and my children) that if your magick doesn't work, if your spiritual plan fails, you should not lose confidence in yourself. Spirit knows what you need and what you don't need, and sometimes, when you are least expecting it, Spirit will step in and bring your work to a grinding halt. Sometimes Spirit does this to protect us, and other times Spirit knows that we have bigger missions, larger goals, and more important activities that we should be doing.

I've taught my children to ask Spirit during a magickal working "to make the best thing happen for me." This way, you allow Spirit to help guide you in your work and play.

The Dark Side—Magickal People Don't Go There

Prosperity gained from theft, drugs, murder, cheating, or any other type of immoral or illegal source is called tainted money. Tainted money carries negative energy, which can affect your overall prosperity. If a friend offers you a "hot" computer, you are opening yourself up to negative circumstances that you may not see immediately—and that negativity may hit you in an area you don't expect. Perhaps the computer works fine, but your love life goes down the tubes—or worse, you may get very ill.

Open Yourself to Abundance

Don't be afraid to open your arms and accept the abundance of the world around you. It is my firm belief that Spirit didn't send anyone here to be unhappy or poverty stricken. I do believe that we have several missions to accomplish. We may succeed, or we may fail. Around it all, however, I sincerely think that Spirit wants you to enjoy your time on this planet as much as you can. There is no reason why you cannot do good work for others and be happy too! Let me whisper something to you, if you don't mind:

**The secret to great prosperity magick
is to let go of your fear.**

How to Use This Book

I've broken prosperity magick into two sections: manifesting abundance and banishing poverty. You can start at the beginning of the book and work through all the abundance spells and then tackle the banishing part, or you can flip back and forth, matching your work to the phases of the moon. The choice is yours. You can also pick and choose which spells you would like to try by themselves, or you can work through them as they are presented in the book, creating your own practical, spiritual, magickal plan. It's entirely up to you!

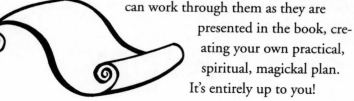

2
Go!
Creating Abundance

You've probably toyed with subconscious ideas about your financial status and overall prosperity for several months before picking up this book. While you were reading the first chapter, your subconscious moved forward, preparing to birth abundance in your life. It's time to take that final step toward manifesting positive abundance. The following spells are to be used from the new moon (the time of beginnings) through the waxing moon (the time of growing), though a few (like the Prosperity Devotion) can be done every day of the month, regardless of the moon phase. You can use only one or two spells, or you can start at the beginning of this chapter and work through to the end, employing all of the spells. It's up to you! Any spell can be done on the full moon, as this is symbolic of the gifts of the Goddess and a time for introspection and power.

At the end of each spell you will find a section entitled *To Enhance This Spell.* These are merely suggestions that may interest the more experienced magickal practitioner, but beginners may wish to try their magickal pinkies at these ideas, too. These spells are designed to bring energies or specific items toward you. Before doing each spell, think carefully about what it is that you truly want. Once you've decided that—go for it!

Prosperity Devotion

In magick and spirituality, a devotion is a simple prayer or meditation done each day with the goal of putting you in a positive frame of mind while connecting to Spirit. Sometimes we worry about money so much that we create negative circumstances in our finances long before they actually take shape as a zero balance in our bank account. My first step into financial well-being began with writing this special devotion to say each morning and evening to help me create positive feelings about myself and my finances.[1]

Supplies: Your brain.

Instructions: Sit quietly in an area without disturbances. Close your eyes. Take three deep breaths. Begin by saying (either mentally or aloud):

At this moment, there is no yesterday.
At this moment, there is no tomorrow.
At this moment, there is only today.
Goddess of abundance, come to me, come to me.

----

1. This spell was inspired by a Debtor's Anonymous technique (check the yellow pages for your local chapter).

Take another deep breath and repeat the last line until you feel yourself relaxing. Say:

I have clothes on my back, food to eat,
and a place to stay.
Goddess of abundance, come to me, come to me.

Continue to repeat the last line until you further relax— until the realization of what you are saying is true. (What if this isn't true? Say it anyway. Verbalizing and thinking of things you wish to manifest in the present tense is an old magickal technique that assists you in bringing your desires into form.) Visualize the things you *do* have, to solidify your words.

Take three more deep breaths, and say:

I am perfectly okay.
Goddess of abundance, come to me, come to me.

Repeat the last line until you relax even further. Now imagine yourself as a strong tree, your roots deep in Mother Earth, your branches and leaves reaching out to Father Sun. Raise your arms if you like, to encourage the visualization. Allow yourself to become part of the God and Goddess energy of the universe. Let go and feel the euphoria. Say:

> **I am one with the universe,**
> **and the universe will provide for me in every way.**
> **Goddess of abundance, come to me, come to me.**

Repeat these lines until you feel an inner calmness wash over you. Open your eyes, and say:

> **At this moment, there is no yesterday, there is**
> **no tomorrow, there is only today. I have clothes**
> **on my back, food to eat, and a place to stay.**
> **I am perfectly okay. I am one with the universe,**
> **and the universe will provide for me in every way.**
> **Goddess of abundance, come to me, come to me.**
> **This is true, as I say. So mote it be!**

Clasp your hands together, hold them out before you, and say: "**In peace.**" Move your hands to the right, and say: "**In harmony.**" Move your hands to the left, and say: "**In truth.**" Bring your hands back to your chest, and say:

**In love. May the Lord and Lady shower
their blessings upon me. I am the source
of my abundance. So mote it be!**

If your financial worries start to get you down throughout the day, go to a quiet place and repeat the above
affirmation.

To enhance this spell:

- Begin at the full moon and perform every day until the
following full moon.

- Begin when the moon first enters the sign of Aries (as
this is a time for spiritual beginnings).

- For seeking a new direction, perform when the moon is
halfway through Aries (no more, as Taurus influences
may steer you toward selfishness).

- Begin on a Sunday in the hour of the sun.[2]

- Perform on Beltaine (May 1) at the rising of the sun.

----

2. If you have never used planetary hours before, don't worry.
There's a complete explanation in appendix 3, pp. 215–218.

Elemental Abundance Spell

Each pool, stream, mountain, lake, rock, comet, well, star, tree, flower, weed, and so on, has its own energy vibration, just as animals and people do. Like vibrations meld together to create a collective unconscious. In the elemental world, these collective energies are known as the sylphs (air), the gnomes (earth), the salamanders (fire), and the undines (water).

Moving through history we find that almost all cultures and civilizations viewed earth, air, water, and fire as the four elements, with this belief first put into focus by the Sumerians. The gnomes, salamanders, sylphs, and undines were considered superhuman in nature, born from the four rivers flowing from the belly of the Great Mother and representing the four fluids of the divine feminine: water, blood, honey, and milk, corresponding to water, fire, air, and earth, respectively. Using this information, I created the following Elemental Abundance Spell.

Supplies: Four small bowls: fill one with water, one with the dragon's blood herb (can substitute red powder or red pepper), one with milk, and one with honey; a picture of yourself.

Instructions: At midday (when the sun is strongest), go outside and draw a pentacle[3] (see next page) in the dirt, sand, or snow with your finger.

At the top of the star, place a representation of yourself (the picture). Going clockwise, place the bowls in the following order: Right arm of pentacle—east; air; honey. Right lower arm of pentacle—south; fire; dragon's blood. Left lower arm of pentacle—west; water. Left upper arm of pentacle—north; earth; milk. As you say the following words, touch each point containing the corresponding element with your hands:

> **Spirit of myself, I call prosperity to myself.**
> **Spirits of the north, by my will and my desire,**
> **I call forth the blessings of the gnomes.**

---

3. The five arms stand for earth, air, fire, water, and the intelligence of the human (top point), surrounded by the spirit of God/dess.

Spirits of the east, by my will and my desire,
I call forth the blessings of the sylphs.
Spirits of the south, by my will and my desire,
I call forth the blessings of the salamanders.
Spirits of the west, by my will and my desire,
I call forth the blessings of the undines.
Spirit of the life force, that which pulses and
surrounds me, I ask for positive abundance
and prosperity in my life. My choices and
possibilities expand every day.

Pentacle

Touch each point again, saying:

Milk, water, blood, and honey *(repeat seven times)*,
I banish all negativity from my body and soul.

Notice you moved in a counterclockwise position with your hands. Then say:

Honey, blood, water, and milk *(seven times)*,
my choices and possibilities expand every day.
With harm to none, so mote it be!

Leave your offering as it stands. Make the following affirmation:

From this day forward, positive abundance
and prosperity flow into my life.
My dreams come true.

To enhance this spell:

• Perform on a Sunday in the hour of the sun or the hour of Jupiter.

- Perform on the new or waxing moon.

- Perform when the moon is in the latter half of Leo, a good time to enhance ambitious personal goals.

- Perform by your garden or favorite yard area.

- Perform during dusk or dawn on Midsummer or Lammas.

Abundance from the Water

For centuries humankind has associated the oceans and rivers of this planet with the cauldron of plenty. Water magick is an incredibly powerful medium, and the fish and mammals that swim in its deep currents carry the essence of the life force. Ancient mystics believed that water was the primary element over the other three (air, earth, and fire), as water came first from the Great  Mother. The concept of the waters of life has been passed from mythos to mythos, and one legend tells us that the goddess Ishtar took the water of life into the underworld to restore Tammuz to life, in keeping with the legends of the goddess' descent. Ishtar is a strong goddess with correspondences including love, sexuality, war, creation, guardianship, healing, and justice, as well as being the overseer of heaven and hell. Ishtar was seen as both a beneficent goddess (the mother of all humans) and a goddess of vibrant power (a warrior goddess who made all other gods tremble in their sandals, therefore earning her the description of "clad in terror"). She is not a goddess to be called on lightly. Ishtar bestows life, bountiful harvest, prosperity, and health. Her planetary correspondence is Venus. Ishtar is a descent goddess, where she is stripped of her worldly possessions and magickal powers in self-sacrifice for the good of another. As with most descent stories, Ishtar returns more powerful than before.

In this spell you will pull Ishtar's energy toward you to create positive abundance in your life and to heal your financial worries using sacred water. Ishtar was called "The Light of the World." Much of the liturgical flattery given to God in the Old Testament of the Bible was directly plagiarized from

Babylonian prayers created for Ishtar.[4] Therefore, should you prefer to use Psalms in your magickal applications, don't feel guilty about the process of changing the "he's" to "she's."

The fish representation in this spell is a worldwide symbol of the Great Mother, consisting of two half moons touching edges, forming the representation of the feminine genitalia. When Rome became Christianized, its citizens were unwilling to give up the Goddess-oriented fish symbolism. These Christians rewrote the mythos surrounding the symbol of the fish to suit this new religion. Earthly female followers of Christ, nuns, received their name from the Hebrew letter (Nun), meaning "fish."

---

4. *The Woman's Encyclopedia of Myth & Secrets,* page 451.

Supplies: One green or blue candle; incense of your choice; a chalice or cup filled with spring water; a flat piece of pliable clay; a stylus, pen, or nail to draw in the clay.

Instructions: Begin this spell on the new or waxing moon. Call on your choice of Divinity or one of the gods or goddesses mentioned above, entreating their assistance. Light the incense and the candle. With your stylus, draw a swimming fish on the clay while thinking of abundance and prosperity swimming into your life. Sprinkle the image with holy water, asking Spirit to bless you with abundance and prosperity. Envision the fish glowing with health and life. Pass the clay over the flame of the candle three times. Hold the fish close to your mouth and blow on the image three times with long, flowing breaths. Then say:

> **I call upon thee, O gracious Ishtar,**
> **She who was known as Light of the World.**
> **I dedicate this rite to You, Ishtar.**
> **You who traveled the descent.**
> **You who brought back the life-giving waters.**

Great Ishtar, I ask for blessings upon this sacred fish
that I have created with my own hands.
Waters of life, I ask for prosperity.
When I cast this clay fish into the waters of
(name the lake, river, or ocean), this fish will draw
into my life-net an abundance of prosperity,
healing, and harmony, in the name of Ishtar.
Waters of life, bring forth my desire. I always have
everything I need, and more. So mote it be!

If you like, you can sing, hum, or meditate, thinking
positive thoughts while holding the fish. When you have
finished, extinguish the candle. Thank deity for assisting
you. Take the water from the chalice and your clay fish
and release them into the waters you named, with the
assurance that prosperity and harmony will manifest
within the month.[5]

Note: Ishtar is not a goddess to be trifled with. Do not
accept money from ill-gotten gains.

---

5. This folk/sympathetic magick spell was originally called "The
Fisherman" and is adapted from *The Grimoire of Lady Sheba*
(Llewellyn Worldwide, 1972).

To enhance this spell:

- Perform on the new or waxing moon.

- Perform on Monday in the hour of the moon.

- Perform when the moon is in Libra, especially if you are seeking abundance through teamwork.

- Perform at midnight.

- Perform on a beach, beside a stream, river, or wishing well.

- Perform at Candlemas (or February 2) using a bowl of melted snow.

Abundance from Fire, Mistletoe, and Oak

Throughout the world—from Australia to South America, from Europe to North America, from Asia to the hidden recesses of Africa—myths abound on the origin of fire. Some claim that the element of fire was a gift from the gods, where other legends indicate that, good humans that we are, we stole this precious commodity from the ancient ones.

British and German folklore cobble the energies of mistletoe, oak, and fire together to form profound rites, spells, and mythos. Mistletoe (a finicky plant) can't be grown in soil. It is a parasitic plant found growing in deciduous trees. Birds carry the seeds of mistletoe to the branches and forks of trees. The most common host tree for the growth of mistletoe is the proud oak. Mistletoe did not figure in Irish Paganism (see *The White Goddess* by Graves), but it does frequent the history of Gaelic Britain and Germany. In Italy and Sweden it was thought that the combination of oak and mistletoe was effective against fire created by lightening. Norse mythology explains that mistletoe was sacred to Baldur. Roman lore equates the plant with the hero Aeneas.

Mistletoe covers quite a few magickal bases, from love, fertility, and immortality to protection and consecration. Here we will use its magickal properties involving birth and purification. Over the years I've discovered that if I'm out of any herbal ingredient, I can substitute mistletoe and still get the results I want. Over the Yule season you'll find me scouring the tri-county area looking for dealers who sell mistletoe (not the fake, plastic stuff). I use this little cache sparingly during the year until I can replenish my supply the following Yule. A little bit of mistletoe in any spell goes a long way. If you have access to mistletoe in the wild, magickal legend indicates that it should be gathered on the first day after a full moon or on Midsummer's Eve or Day, and that the herb should never touch the ground.

Fire is an element of purification, and if we add the oak chips and mistletoe, we can produce a powerful spell for prosperity. Among American Indian tribes in the Eastern United States (Shawnee, Fox, and other Central Algonquians), the smoke created by the fire was thought to carry the words of prayers up to the supreme deity. Before offering any invocation, a small amount of tobacco or a mixture of special herbs was placed on the fire to validate the prayer.[6] In this spell we will send the message of our needs to the goddess Vesta through the medium of smoke.

----

6. *Standard Dictionary of Folklore, Mythology, and Legend.*
   Funk & Wagnall, 1984. Page 390.

Vesta, a Roman goddess, governed household affairs, ceremonies, mother magick, and household guardians. She was worshiped daily, especially at meals, and her temples contained the eternal fires, which were replenished on March 1, while her festival of honor occurred on June 1. Unlike other goddesses and gods who had statues in the shrines of the people, Vesta's true embodiment was the fire itself. These fires were thought to be the mystical heart of the empire. Where the opening praise of the god Janus began each service, the closing praise belonged to Vesta (where we derive the word *vesper*). Although there were no images of the goddess in her own temple, statues of her in Rome were prevalent. She was often portrayed clothed and veiled, holding a chalice, torch, scepter, and palladium (a small, sacred object seen as a fetish or statue). In A.D. 382, the endowments of all the pagan temples were withdrawn, including that of Vesta's 700-year-old Mother-hearth, but the idea of the

Vesta symbol

eternal sacred flame was adopted by the Christians and used in various aspects of their worship (minus the vestal virgins, of course).

Supplies: One charcoal grill; fast-lighting charcoal; ¹⁄₁₆ ounce mistletoe; a handful of oak wood chips; one black marker; prosperity incense. Before you begin the spell, draw the symbol of Vesta (see previous page) on each wood chip with the black marker.

Instructions: Not only does this spell work well during the new and waxing moons, it also does a bang-up job if performed on the full moon. Set an old grill on your patio or in your yard. Cense the area with your favorite prosperity incense. Place five pieces of quick-lighting charcoal on the center of the grate. Draw a pentacle over the coals in the air. Sprinkle mistletoe and a handful of oak chips over the coals. As long as the fire burns, chant:

> **Goddess Vesta of the holy fire,**
> **sacred smoke lifting higher,**
> **herbs of oak and mistletoe,**
> **work the magick, help it go.**

**By thy light glowing,
by fortune growing,
bring to me prosperity,
inner peace, love, and joy.
With harm to none, so mote it be!**

When the ashes cool, put a little in a bottle and bring into the house. Renew every six months by offering the ashes to the winds and replacing with new.

To enhance this spell:

- Perform on a Sunday in the hour of the sun.

- Perform at midday.

- Perform when the moon is in Sagittarius if your plan for abundance calls for travel, a sporting adventure, or if you wish to have an honest and direct interchange with someone who can move you along on your path.

- Perform in the early stages of the moon in Virgo if your spellwork is associated with the home.

- Perform by a fire pit.

- Perform at Midsummer (June 21).

Abundance from the Earth

Like several ancient goddesses, the Roman goddess Fortuna
(*Tyche* in Greek) has many faces, presiding over the fertility of
the earth and its inhabitants. Her primary sign of the zodiac
is Virgo. Fortuna stands on a globe (representing the earth),
holding a cornucopia in one hand from which she strews luck
and abundance on those she favors. In some instances she was
thought to steer the affairs of the world. As Fortuna Vir-
ginensis, she protected newly married women and helped
them to remain beautiful and alluring to their husbands. As
Fors Fortuna, she was a goddess of luck. Fortuna is often
veiled or blindfolded. Her symbol is the wheel of fortune,
representing her title of "She Who Turns the Year." Fortuna
Augusti was the foundation of the emperor's right to rule the
Roman Empire. As a daughter of Jupiter, along with her associations with luck, abundance, and prosperity, her correspondences include the planet Jupiter and Thursday. Odd numbers are sacred to Fortuna. One can turn to her to banish or
embellish one's circumstances. Fortuna's feast day is June 11.
This goddess continued to have a prominent place in the

Christian Middle Ages, appearing in Latin, German, and French poetry and songs. She is definitely a goddess of the earth and cares deeply about its people.

Another element in our spell, cinnamon, finds its history in ancient China, where the herb was used for temple purification and prosperous ventures. Cinnamon comes from the aromatic inner bark of a tree in the laurel family. This spice was first mentioned in Chinese writings in 2700 B.C. and we find further reference to its use in conjunction with religious rites in historical information associated with Jewish and Arab tribal functions. At one point cinnamon was ranked in value with gold and frankincense. Today, cinnamon is considered "the" herb for money magick.

By the time I began writing this Earth Abundance Spell, my other spells for abundance were working so well, I was really on a roll. Unfortunately, I forgot that I lived with other people (my children particularly)—and they always have some unusual need that's got to be met "right away, Mom!" To combat these emergency needs, I put together the following magickal working that I could do throughout the month, no matter what the moon phase.

Supplies: One small container of cinnamon; a thin spindle (the kind they stick cash register receipts on—I once used a candle holder with a prong because I couldn't find a spindle); three one-dollar bills.

Instructions: Beginning on a Thursday in the hour of Jupiter (as close to the new moon as possible), place one dollar bill on the spindle. Sprinkle with cinnamon. Hold your hands over the dollar bill, and say:

> **Veiled Fortuna, goddess of luck,**
> **sweet sister of fortune,**

spinner of the Wheel of Destiny,
grant me the gift of prosperity.
Bring me the blessings of positive abundance.
With harm to none, so mote it be!

Place the second dollar bill on top of the first, sprinkle with cinnamon, and say:

Spirits of earth, element of prosperity,
strong Mother of my fortune,
grant me the gift of unlimited resources.
Bring me the blessings of positive abundance.
With harm to none, so mote it be!

Place the third dollar bill on top of the second, sprinkle with cinnamon, and say:

I am fortunate.
I am successful.
I am positive abundance.
I am prosperity. So mote it be!

Before you go to bed in the evening, add a dollar bill or two on top of the pile. Don't forget to sprinkle with cinnamon and say the last affirmation ("**I am prosperity**"). When your spindle is full, remove all but the first dollar bill and start over again. Put the dollars in a special bank account or in a magick money box to save for a rainy day. If for some reason you have to use all the money, repeat the entire spell, beginning with a new dollar bill. As the money on the spindle increases, so will your personal finances. My cash flow picked up considerably with this spell. Then, when my kids had to have money one morning for something at school, I gave it to them because it was all I had in the house. (I can remember my daughter wrinkling her nose and saying, "What's with all the dust?") The only mistake I made was to give her *all* the money—I forgot to leave the last dollar on the spindle. My cash flow dropped immediately. I quickly re-did the spell and remembered the next time to leave that last dollar there!

To enhance this spell:

• If your spell requires exactness to build money for a particular need, perform when the moon is in Virgo or Capricorn.

- Perform on Thursday in the hour of Jupiter.

- Spell preparation works well when the moon is moving from Taurus into Gemini, but under a Taurus moon people are usually unwilling to lend money, so this is a poor time for banking matters.

- Perform at dusk.

- Perform in a circle of standing stones.

- Perform at Beltaine (May 1).

Abundance from the Air

From the strong winds of change, to the gentle breezes of movement, to the use of holy breath, air magick can clean out those dusty cobwebs of procrastination, reverse a negative aspect or influence, or push along a project in the right direction. Like a small breeze that can coalesce into a mighty front, we are going to use an ancient technique called the cumulative spell that employs repetition, a basic characteristic of many folk enchantments. In the cumulative spell, a new element is added to the original simple statement, and the growing list is recited after each addition (much like the song "The Twelve Days of Christmas"). Done preferably at the new moon, you are free to choose which day or planetary hour you desire. The only supply you will need is a bell.

The bell has served various religious functions all over the world, including Assyrian practices in 600 B.C., Chinese temple bells, Babylonian worship, Egyptian feasts, aborigine invocations, Hindu rites, and invocations by Haitian vouduns. To date, no one can pinpoint exactly when the bell entered human culture. Bells have been used for a variety of purposes, including amulets, fertility charms, a summons to deity, prophecy, curative agents, and of course as a musical instrument. Europeans rang bells to thwart the power of a thunderstorm and break the oncoming storm front. In this spell we use the bell to summon Divinity and the elements as well as to ward off negativity.

Instructions: Hold your hands over the bell and ask Divinity for prosperity and protection. You can choose a favorite deity if you like. I simply used the word "Divinity" to keep the spell simple. This spell is to be done facing east (the position of air) at dawn (or when you arise from a night's sleep—I realize we've got second and third shifters these days). Begin by saying: **"I call forth Divinity."** Ring the bell, and say: **"I call forth the prosperity and protection of the element of earth. I magnetize the positive things I need and want to come to me. Now!"** Ring the bell. Now say:

> **This is the spell**
> **that works so well**
> **that starts with a bell** (*ring the bell*)
> **that brings a smile**
> **that breaks the trial**
> **that sweeps the room**
> **and clears out doom.**
> **That creates abundance**
> **powered by redundancy**
> **which brings prosperity.**

Not only does this spell work, it is an excellent word game for your children or coven mates. To help you out, it goes something like this:

1 This is the spell, that works so well, this is the spell.

2 This is the spell, that works so well, that starts with a bell *(ring the bell)*, that works so well, this is the spell.

3 This is the spell, that works so well, that starts with a bell, that brings a smile, that starts with a bell *(ring the bell)*, that works so well, this is the spell.

4 This is the spell, that works so well, that starts with a bell, that brings a smile, that breaks the trial, that brings a smile, that starts with a bell *(ring the bell)*, that works so well, this is the spell . . . and so on. Whew!

Note: At the end of the spell you can say specifically what it is that you want, then ring the bell.

To enhance this spell:

• Perform at dawn.

• Perform when the moon is in Gemini if you desire dramatic change.

- Perform on Friday in the hour of Venus.

- Perform on a cliff, bluff, or other high place where the wind is always present.

- Perform at Ostara (Spring Equinox).

Abundance from the Huntress

The primary goddess in this spell is Artemis, the Greek hunting goddess who is also equated with the Roman Diana. Originally an Amazonian moon goddess, Artemis' name was shortened by the Helvetians, who called her Artios—hence the Celtic association of Artemis and Artios. Seen as the protectress of wild animals, the newly born, lakes, rivers, forests, the moon, and night, Artemis will also help you hunt for prosperity. The first fruits of a harvest or the catch of a hunt were hung on trees in acceptance of her patronage and blessings. Her totem animals are the bear (healing) and the wolf (family and clan activity). At Artemis' shrine in Arcadia, girls between five and ten years of age, called "brown bears," would dance in her honor at feasts and celebrations.

Artemis is the goddess of the loud chase, the slayer of stags, the archer who travels through the shadowy hills and windy headlands in breathless anticipation of her goal, holding her golden bow ready for the kill. She was Orthia (upright) and Lygodesma (willow-bound), Agrotera (huntress), Coryphaea (of the peak), Limnaea (of the lake), Daphnaea (of the laurel), Lyceia (of the wolf), Aeginaea (of the goat), Caryastis (of the walnut tree), Ariste (best), and Calliste (fairest). Her temple was one of the seven wonders of the ancient world. For those of you who seek your German roots, Artemis/Diana was known as Dea Abnoba, patron of the Black Forest. In this spell we are going to use an invocation that includes some of the names attributed to Artemis energy.

The wolf figures prominently in New World and European lore with both positive and negative associations. First seen as a manifestation of the divine and a totem to many gods, goddesses, and human families, the wolf legends became less positive with European superstition and the creation of the werewolf mythos. The wolf fared well, however, in the New World legends. Should you prefer to use a god for this spell, there are plenty to choose from that work well with the wolf: Zeus (Greco-Roman), Apollo (Greco-Roman), Anubis (Egyptian), and Cernunnos (Romano-Celtic). Some Irish tribes claimed the wolf as their spiritual father or ghost father. They wore wolf skins and used wolves' teeth for amulets. Germanic tribes believed that if they wore the wolf skin, their warriors would turn into wolves, gifted with the power to defeat their enemies. The wolf is a strong, family-based totem energy, concentrating on unity and prosperity for the clan.

Supplies: Incense of your choice; chalice or cup filled with spring water; a dish filled with dirt; a chunk of pliable clay; a stylus, pen, or nail to draw in the clay; string; thirteen thin green ribbons, thirteen inches long; thirteen tiny bells; one green candle.

Instructions: Call on Artemis, entreating her assistance. Light the incense and the candle. With your hands, form a wolf out of part of the clay while thinking of abundance and prosperity moving into your life. With the rest of the clay, form three arrows. Carve your name

with the stylus on the belly of the wolf, then carve your
desire, using either words or pictures, on the arrows.
After the clay dries, sprinkle with a few drops of the
spring water (do not add salt) and the dirt, asking Spirit
to bless you with abundance and prosperity. Envision
the wolf and arrows glowing with health and life. Pass
the wolf and arrows over the flame of the candle three
times. Hold the wolf and the arrows close to your mouth
and blow on the images three times with long, flowing
breaths. Then say:

I call upon thee, O gracious Artemis,
queen of the moon, goddess of wisdom.
I dedicate this rite to you. I ask for blessings
upon this sacred wolf and these arrows
that I have created with my own hands.
When I leave this wolf and the arrows
in my yard *(or the forest)*, this wolf will draw
into my life an abundance of prosperity,
healing, and harmony. The arrows are my gift
to Artemis, that she may continue to enjoy

her wild hunt with the golden bow
as her familiar wolf runs by her side.
I affirm my right to prosperity. So mote it be!

You can sing, hum, or meditate, thinking positive thoughts, while holding the wolf. Try chanting the many names of Artemis: "**Artemis, Diana, Devana—Tauro, Artios, Dea Abnoba**" (you can select any of her names and string them together in a chant). Tie a bell on the end of each ribbon. Tie the ribbons together, intoning the Artemis chant, then tie the ribbons securely around the belly of the wolf. When you have finished, extinguish the candle. Thank deity for assisting you. Release the circle. Take the water from the chalice, the dirt, your clay wolf and arrows, and walk into your yard. Hang the clay animal (with the string wrapped securely around its stomach) from a tree. Pour the water and the dirt at the base of the tree beside the small arrows you will leave there as your offering. Ask for one final blessing, knowing that prosperity and harmony will manifest within the month. Call to the gnomes, saying:

**Gnomes of the wood
treasure abound
bring me wealth from Artemis' ground.**

Leave the wolf in the tree.

To enhance this spell:

- Perform on a new moon.

- Perform in the hour of Jupiter, or
  on a Sunday or Thursday.

- Perform at midnight.

- Perform when the moon is in Sagittarius.

- Perform during the Hunter's Moon.

- Perform at Mabon (Fall Equinox).

Abundance from the Ancestors

The dead, especially those who have personally loved you, are
not powerless. This particular ceremony contains great

beauty, peace, and harmony—very good when you're a bit vexed about your financial condition.

In this spell we make use of the sacred rattle, which has such a long history we could read about it all day and still not be done. Different cultures associated the rattle with various magickal techniques, but the most common uses were to dispel negativity and to call on mystical spirits, such as totem animals or the ancestral dead. From wire (the Egyptian sistrum) to gourds (Native American), the rattle has been used to bring healing and prosperity while banishing negative forces.

In this spell we invoke the energies of those who loved us; however, I would like to include that Santerians believe you should invoke the assistance of the ancestor who didn't like you much in life, or who treated you badly, as they really need to work off the bad karma. By asking for their help, you are allowing them to pay you back with positive energy.

Although there are many feminine deities associated with the land of the dead, for this spell I've chosen Barinthus, the mysterious otherworldly Welsh sea god, whose responsibility lies in ferrying the dead across the vast seas of time to the Summerland.

Supplies: One purple pillar candle (purple is often associated with the higher mind and the energy of the dead); seven white votive candles (for purity of intent); a picture of the individual or individuals who loved you and who have passed away (you can also add something that belonged to them, such as a piece of jewelry, a favorite book, or other keepsake); one black and one white feather (for balance); an offering for the dead that includes something from the earth or sea; your favorite incense; your desire, written on a piece of green paper (or on white paper with a green-inked pen); a rattle (to banish negativity and call the dead).

Instructions: Place your desire-paper (called a *petition*) under the purple candle. Around this candle, place the seven white votive candles. Around these candles, place the picture of the ancestor, covered by the black and white feathers, your offering of gifts from the earth or sea, and the incense.

Visualize a circle of white light around you. Light the incense. State your desire aloud. Call Barinthus to carry the deceased to the circle on his boat of light, if this be the will of the gods. Light the purple candle, stating who you wish to call and the desire you wish to manifest. Light the white votive candles in honor of the deceased, saying their name aloud. Speak about the gifts that they gave you in life and offer them your thanks and blessings.

Sit quietly. Again visualize the white light around you. Close your eyes. Shake your rattle slowly and softly. Call out the deceased's name, and ask them to hear your desire. Always be honest and frank in your words. Repeat your desire in a sing-song voice (the communication line between yourself and the dead is not always clear, so you want to make sure they hear exactly what it is that you want). Mentally visualize your desire while you continue to shake your rattle. Stop when you lose the visualization.

Put your hands over the purple candle (not too close!) and say:

> **I call the dead to bond my spell.**
> **Air speed its travel well,**
> **Fire give it Spirit, strength, and love;**
> *(Deceased's name),* **grant this petition from above.**[7]

----

7. Chant credited to the late Scott Cunningham.

Gaze into the candle flame and visualize your desire
manifesting. Relax. Take a deep breath. Thank the
deceased for assisting you. Ask Barinthus to guide the
deceased loved one back to the Summerland. Thank
Barinthus. Allow the candles to continue burning until
almost nothing is left of them. Keep the candle ends
until your desire has manifested, then bury them on
your property. Place your offering at a special place in
your yard.

To enhance this spell:

- Perform on the full moon.

- Perform on Monday (family love) in
  the hour of Saturn (the planetary hour
  of the dead).

- Perform at 3:00 A.M. (the daily hour
  of the dead).

- Perform on Samhain, All Soul's
  Day, or All Saint's Day.

Angel Spell for Abundance

I've found angel magick to be an incredible, positive vehicle in various magickal applications. The history of angelic presence predates Judaism and Christianity. Indeed, our Pagan ancestors employed these messenger-spirits in much of their primitive spirituality. Some of you with Pagan associations may not like this spell, thinking that the angelic names are entirely Christian. I've found, however, that many angelic names predate Judaism and Christianity and find their roots in the Sumerian and Chaldean mythos.

In this spell we use the concept of mnemonic verse. There are similar patterns in Hebrew Scripture (Psalm 119, which consists of twenty-two eight-verse sections corresponding to the twenty-two letters of the Hebrew alphabet) and the earliest extant English rhyme, dating from c.1375, which is Chaucer's *ABC,* an homage to the Blessed Virgin (taken from a French original written a half-century before). In studying the folklore and magick of the Pennsylvania Dutch (German-Americans), I found shorter versions—evidently they felt that only the first few lines were needed in their magickal incantations, rather than the whole alphabet. Here we are going to stick with the original mnemonic idea by using twenty-four angelic names, thereby producing an Angel Spell for Abundance.

Instructions: This spell can be said anytime. Works well by accentuating with a rattle or drum. Can be done in group form, where one person says a line, and then the line is repeated by the group, followed by the word "Ho!"

(Say your intention:) _____

Ariel begins it.

Baradiel guides it.

The Chalkydri sing it.

Devas manifest it.

Elohim wills it.

The Fravashi better it.

Gabriel brings it.

The Hafaza watch it.

The Ischim balance it.

Jael guards it.

Kadmiel births it.

Lahabiel aids it.

Michael raises it.

Nebo ministers it.

Ofaniel sees it.

Patron angels devote it.

The Queen of angels speaks it.

Raphael inspires it.

Sandalphon prays it.

Thrones sanctify it.

Uriel strengthens it

Vrevoil reveals it.

Watchers protect it.

Xathanael patrons it.

Yahriel places the glory of the moon on it.

Zodiac angels seal it.

And Spirit brings it through time and space.

So be it. Ho!

Seal in the air with the sigil of the equal-armed cross
(see next page) using your dominant hand or rattle.
(Just to reassure you, I double-checked all the angelic
correspondences and tried not to choose any that have

Equal-armed cross

unfortunately had their names sullied through historical misrepresentation.)[8]

If you would prefer a more Paganized version using Western European deities, try this one:

Aradia begins it.
Brigid fuels it.
Cerridwen magicks it.
Dagda manifests it.
Echo repeats it.

----

8. You can find this information in *Angels A to Z—A Who's Who of the Heavenly Host* by Matthew Bunson. Crown Trade Paperbacks, New York. 1996.

Epona protects it.
Gwen smiles upon it.
Habonde grows it.
Inghean Bhuide blesses it.
Japheth powers it.
Korrigan feeds it.
LoBan beautifies it.
Melusine raises it.
Nair ministers it.
Olwen shines upon it.
Phlox brings all elements to it.
The Queen of Angels speaks it.
Rhiannon bestows charisma upon it.
Scota prays it.
The Triple Goddesses sanctify it.
Urganda strengthens it.
Veleda reveals it.
The Wyrds protect it.
Ygerna places the glory of the moon on it.
Zadan seals it.
And Spirit brings it through time and space.
So be it. Ho!

To enhance this spell:

• Perform outdoors under a starry sky.

• Perform when the moon is in Leo to gain the generosity of others.

• Perform on Sunday in the hour of Venus.

• Perform on Christmas, December 21 (Yule), or New Year's Day.

Circle Round Abundance Meditation

I'll give you a break from history and legend. The following little meditation has really helped me. On any day or evening, from the new to full moon, sit quietly and close your eyes. Relax. See yourself as the energy of prosperity. *Be* the energy of prosperity. Chant, or repeat in your mind:

**Circle, circle, round round;
round round, circle round.**

Then calm and center yourself, thinking of yourself as the energy of success and prosperity. *Be* the energy of prosperity.

This spell is a terrific one to do anytime, and is especially helpful when those financial worries start to get you down.

To enhance this spell:

- Load a green candle with cinquefoil, mint, and vervain (see page 185 for loading); burn.

- Perform on a full moon in the hour of Jupiter.

- Drum or use a rattle while intoning the spell.

- Perform on January 1 (New Year's Day) or on your birthday.

Abundance from American Magick

According to family records, my ancestors arrived in America from Germany in the late 1600s. They became part of the Pennsylvania Dutch heritage in the counties of York, Adams, and Cumberland. I'm proud to say they never owned slaves and were basically a hard-working bunch, though on the southern side I'm directly descended from a tent revivalist with fourteen children and a still owner in Hackers Creek, West Virginia. (Oh well, that was the Scottish side of the family and I'm proud of them just the same.) On the Northern side, my German ancestors quickly learned how to use their personalized folk magick, Pow-Wow, to their advantage, including the popular hex signs that continue to hold their popularity today.[9]

Pictured on the next page is the hex sign for abundance and good will for all. This typical eight-pointed star has associations with angelic energies. The large star is usually depicted in blue, with four red tulips rising between alternating star points. The large star stands for protection, good luck, and good fortune. A second, smaller eight-point star forms the design center, done in alternating red and black. The red stands for the power of the sun and the power of one's lineage. The black stands for the gifts of the earth and protection against negativity. The blue singular, smaller stars and green wheat symbolize abundance and good will, where the red tulips represent faith and trust as well as the cauldron of positive transformation. Tulips are seen as "Witches' Feet," going back to the symbolism of the God of the Forest and his

---

9. You can obtain pre-painted hex signs from Jacob Zook's Hex Shops, Inc., P. O. Box 104, Paradise, PA, 17562.

Hex Sign

cloven hoof. The outer circle, painted in green, holds the abundance energies together to focus power and protect your home and property. Place this sign on your altar when working for abundance and good will. Burn a brown candle to influence friendly energies.

Supplies: Hex sign; parchment paper; colored pencils, markers, or paints in blue, red, black, and green; a brown candle; spring water; money oil of your choice; rattle or drum.

Instructions: On the new moon, draw the hex sign (see previous page) on a piece of parchment paper (white paper is okay if you can't find any parchment, though it might be worth your while to check out a local art store and pick up a roll, as there are all sorts of spells you can cobble together using parchment). You can also use a white paper plate or a circle of wood painted with a base coat of white. With colored pencils, markers, or paints, color the design.

Determine what type of abundance you desire. For example, if you want an abundance of family love, then choose Sunday, Monday, or Friday to energize your hex sign. If you are interested in personal power, Tuesday would be the day of choice. Abundance in money, property, and business corresponds with Thursday, and if you are looking more toward communication issues, then Wednesday would be the best choice. Pick your planetary hour with the same procedure in mind.

Sprinkle the hex sign's back with spring water. Energize by holding your hands over the sign and asking Divinity for blessings. Seal the empowerment with the money oil of your choice on the back of the hex sign with an equal armed cross (page 56). You can use the prosperity oil recipe found in this book (page 84) or you can purchase an oil from a magickal shop. Money oils usually run between three and seven dollars, depending on the ingredients. If you can't get a money oil, olive oil or almond oil will do. I usually touch each tulip and each star with the money oil also.

Hold your hands over the hex sign, chanting: **"Prosperity, come to me,"** three times. Then take your rattle or drum and continue until you tire, saying:

With harm to none. My will is done. So mote it be!

Carry the hex sign to each quarter (N, S, E, W), asking the elements to give their blessings. Visualize each quarter's energy filling the hex sign. Hold the hex sign aloft, asking Spirit for blessings as well. Hang the sign in a prominent place in your home. Re-energize every new moon.

To enhance this spell:

- The primary colors of the American Pow-Wow were red, white, and black: red for the blood of heritage, white for purity, and black for the richness of the earth and protection. Burn candles in these colors while invoking the energies of the hex sign.

- Perform when the moon is in Leo for vitality, or when the moon is in Virgo for matters of the home.

- Perform at Lammas (August 2) or during the full moon in August.

- Perform in the sign of Leo (the Pow-Wow's favorite spellcasting window), July 21 to August 21.

3

Manifesting Wealth

Time to do some serious thinking on your financial goals, especially where those goals relate to specific items. In the last chapter we worked with general abundance, though you could change any of those spells to enhance a particular project, should you so desire. In this chapter we'll concentrate on specifics, such as your personal money flow, manifesting large-ticket items, enhancing your bank balance, and other financial enterprises.

We'll also talk a little about project building and our relationships with others concerning our prosperity.

As with the last chapter, the manifesting spells presented here generally correspond with the new moon (to manifest beginnings) through the waxing moon (the time to add growth energies). Again, the full moon is used for inspiration and power. I've also included the "end pieces" for each spell, filled with suggestions for those who would like to try the spell with a more complicated twist.

The Group Mind

I've discovered that the group mind of your family and close friends relates to your health and financial success. If one member of the family is a hypochondriac, then you can bet many family members have a habit of thinking up diseases for themselves, even if they don't vocalize their fears. If one person suffers from abuse, the whole family suffers. Nothing—no pain, no sorrow, no happiness, no joy—comes to any one person alone. Your financial status works the same way. If your parents always worried about money and talked constantly of being poor, then you (as an adult) may think

that way, too (I came from this category). This negative
thought process drew negative energy into the family
finances. Repeated statements of how poor you are provide a
nasty cauldron of failure. When I was a kid, I was always
told, "Bakers (that was my last name) never have any
money." I heard that statement so often, I believed it. I strug-
gled through many years of this kind of negative thinking
and very tough financial times, especially when my kids were
very young.

Although all magickal applications rely on your belief in a
positive future, I've found prosperity magick requires that you
let go of all negative inhibitions (thoughts and feelings) you
may have had about money in the past. You need to open
your arms and accept the abundance of wealth. This is,
indeed, a choice. *Visualize prosperity as an energy in and of
itself—an energy of which there is more than enough for everyone.*

I've also discovered that panic is a terrible epidemic, especially in a closed, family environment, when you're talking
about money. I'd been working prosperity magick for over a
year and everything was perking along just fine. Suddenly,
from out of the proverbial-blue-of-money-sucking-land, a

large bill squatted firmly in the family lap. Normally I'm the one who panics and my husband is the calm one. Not this time. He ranted and raved. He paced the floor. He did the "how will we?" syndrome. (How will we survive? How will we pay this now? How will we pay something else later? If I'd only known I wouldn't have spent . . . you get the picture, right?) His panic was contagious and soon we were all in a tizzy. Kitchen-sinking began. (You know, dredging up old emotional wounds that haven't healed properly?) I found myself back in that awful emotional state I'd been in before I started seriously working on my financial well-being.

The difference this time was that a part of me watched what was happening with a cold, logical eye, and I realized that things were not as bad as they seemed. This was just a minor setback (or even a lesson well learned). I concentrated on calming my husband down, and every time he brought up something negative from the past, I gently told him "You don't want to go there, that has no bearing on the issue at hand," and then proceeded to do the magickal work necessary to enhance our financial affairs so I could pay that bill without hardship. It worked, and we both learned something from the experience.

While you work prosperity magick, think long and hard about your previous and current environment. Consciously separate yourself from negative physical and emotional patterning. Learn to heal old wounds that are coupled with financial issues.

The Ebb and Flow of Your Money [1]

I learned a long time ago that our lives ebb and flow with the energy of the seasons. I also discovered that each individual has a personal cycle that includes busy times and fallow times that may have nothing to do with seasonal energies, planetary influences, or moon phases. These cycles are healthy and normal. It wasn't much of a stretch, then, to conclude that this energy movement within our lives also affects the ebb and flow of our prosperity. Other things in our lives also undulate in cycles: relationships, emotions, sleep patterns,

---

1. The concept of money-in and money-out came from Sanaya Roman and Duane Packer's book *Creating Money, Keys to Abundance* (see Bibliography). I recommend this book for those who are budget-conscious.

and so on. As one part of our daily life rises to excellence, something else may falter or slow without our conscious observance. If these cycles are natural, then how are we to cope—especially when we're talking about cold, hard cash?

First, learn your personal cycle. Sit down and go over the ebb and flow of your money within one month, and then within the year. If you're the step-by-step kind of gal or guy, you might want to make a graph with colored pencils to help you pinpoint days when you emotionally reach that "critical" stage. Creatively consider how you could bring balance into this natural ebb and flow. Second, learn to control the negative emotions that you associate with those natural fallow times. Seek out positive activities over those few days (or weeks). You may discover several peaks and valleys in your chart, or perhaps only a few. Everyone is different.

Does this mean that you will definitely be poor some days and rich others? No. This just means that energy cycles will be different, and you need to become attuned to these personal cycles, then act appropriately. By working through the abundance spells and banishing spells (in the next chapter), you will already have started this, assuming that you've already jumped around a bit in the book to find those spells that would immediately meet your needs; if you haven't done this, that's okay, too.[2]

In a twenty-eight-day lunar cycle, we know that there is a time for drawing things toward you (the new to full moon) and a time to push negative energies away from you (full to new moon). We know, too, that the full moon is often considered a period of balance, where both manifesting and banishing practices will work well. We also know that you have a personal cycle that may (or may not) adhere to the lunar cycle, the seasons, or planetary influences. How do we get all these energies to work together to create positive abundance? Actually, it's not that hard, once you put your noggin to work.

What kind of energy is moving about you today? Is money flowing in at a steady pace or is there more going out the door? Perhaps this is an even day (or week)—nothing in, nothing out.

Money In—This is great, but don't sabotage yourself like I used to do. Money would come in, things would be great, and I would be busy. Sometimes I thought I was too busy, so I

---

2. If you are really into magickal timing, you might want to have an astrologer take a peek at your natal chart.

would sit and contemplate that events should slow a bit until I got a handle on things. I literally projected things stopping. Mistake. After a few days, more money would go out than in. I'd subconsciously dammed my monetary flow. On the days of monetary flow (money in), keep those creative fires burning. Continue your abundance or banishing work. Look at money as energy. Give this energy a color, if you like (green is an obvious choice). Concentrate on this energy continuing to grow all around you.

Money Out—More money going out than coming in leads to depression. To remind myself that money-out days are only temporary, I started to do something special on them—something to make my day different. Sometimes I would play games with my children, take a walk, or read a good book. I made darned sure I did something magickal, even if it was just cleaning my altar, learning something new, tidying up my magickal cabinet (a day-long job in itself), or rearranging items on one of my household shrines. I discovered that a small bit of magick will lift your spirits and help you get through a trying day. Try a long, ritual bath, an invigorating shower, or a bit of gardening to get you in touch with the earth.

Repeat positive affirmations or do a little meditation. I could give you an incredibly long list of things that I've tried—and all of them worked. Remember that money-out days are a *temporary* condition that will lessen in intensity and length as you learn to manifest abundance in your life.

Money-out days (or weeks) can mean that you've got a block somewhere and it's time to start searching through your lifestyle to figure out where that block is and what you're going to do about it. Some blocks can be removed within seconds (like a pesky, negative thought), where others may not be so easy (like a spouse who can't keep their paws off the twenty-four-hour cash machine). Blocks can be mental, emotional, physical, or spiritual. Only you, the master sleuth of your life, can determine what those blocks might be. Sometimes the blocks will be self-imposed and other times the blocks will be created by others.

For years, I had an energy block regarding money-out days. Different though, from years past, was my new determination to be prosperous. I'd worked through a lot of negative things and accomplished a great deal, yet I was in a backslide—more money-out than money-in. As I worked through all the spells in this book, I had fewer and fewer money-out days and lots more money-in days. Once I began the concerted effort to become prosperous, any blocks I'd experienced in the past began to crumble and I was well on my way to the lifestyle that I wanted.

Nothing in, nothing out—I used to find these days incredibly frustrating (and frightening) if I had just gone through a money-out period, but during a money-in period I found these inactive times quiet and calming. Either way, these days are *not* the days to sit on your magickal you-know-what and watch the hours slip by. No, no, no! Nothing in, nothing out may mean that you aren't clear on what you really want, which is a normal human condition. Most people are afraid to reach for what they most desire because they rationalize (for whatever reason) that it just can't happen. On these days, work on something that you would *like* to do (not what you think you *must* or *should* do). It was on a nothing in, nothing out day that I came up with the following Golden Cord of Manifestation exercise. Now, it took me a while to master this exercise, so don't throw your hands up in despair if it doesn't work for you right away. Just keep at it. Eventually the technique will get easier and easier.

Note: Some folks, by nature, prefer passivity. I'm one of those people. When things perk along and I experience money-in times, I forget to work for future abundance. I become complacent with the world and everything in it. If I'm getting too comfortable, Spirit often hits me upside the head, saying: "Time to get moving. Let's have a money-out week just to keep you on your magickal toes."

The Golden Cord of Manifestation

Although gold hasn't always been hard to obtain, its ability to resist tarnish and remain consistently pleasing to the eye has made it popular in various cultures throughout history. Reminiscent of the greater lights (our sun and the stars), religious worship often linked gold to deity. Mythos include the Greek and Roman Golden Age, the golden apples of Hesperides (Greek), the golden bough (Roman), the tale of the golden cockerel (Russian), the golden fleece (Greek), the golden stool (African), and the Golden Legend (the process of compiling the lives of the saints). The Golden Rule (do unto others as you would have them do unto you) is referenced in Egyptian, Akkadian, and Buddhist writings, dated 500 years before the Christian scriptures. In some cases (Egyptian), the rule was associated with goddess worship (sacred to Maat). Gold is a particular favorite of the Santerian goddess Oshun, prosperity deity of streams and rivers.

The following is more of an exercise than it is a spell. You'll need to practice to become proficient. That's okay. A little work is good for the soul, and keeps you from getting bored.

Supplies: A golden thread or cord that is the length of your body height; a small empty matchbox painted gold or yellow; a slip of paper that will fit into the box; a gold-inked pen or gold-leaded pencil; a golden candle (white will do as a substitute).

Instructions: Hold your hands over the supplies and ask for blessings in the name of your chosen deity for the purpose of prosperity. On the piece of paper, write something that you wish to manifest. It can be a large or small item or goal. (Remember, bigger things usually take longer to manifest.) Hold the paper and blow on it three times. Put the paper in the box.

Tie one end of the cord around the box. Hold the gold candle in your hand and think about what you want to manifest, then think of how you felt at a time when you had what you wanted. In your mind, link that emotional feeling to the picture of what you wish to manifest now. Light the candle. Try to hold on to that feeling as long as you can.

Close your eyes. Begin running the free end of the cord through your hands while you think about what you want to manifest. Picture yourself drawing your desire through the cord and into your hands. Keep moving the cord through your hands until you get to the box. Hold the box in your hands and continue to think about what you wish to manifest. See yourself happy and holding the desire (or having the energy of the desire around you). Try not to let negative thoughts intrude. Hold the box until you feel your energy rise or feel a slight tingling in your hands. Take a deep breath and open your eyes. Put out the candle.

Repeat this exercise every day until you receive your desire or until twenty-eight days have passed. If you do not have the goal in twenty-eight days, get a fresh candle and begin again. Over the twenty-eight days, be consciously aware of opportunities that may present themselves to you, especially if this is a non-material goal. Be sure to accept those opportunities. Once you have manifested the goal, burn the paper and begin with a new goal or desire. Don't stop after one goal or manifestation. Keep going. This is a great exercise for any student, and can be done in a group format.

Note: Do not work yourself into a tizzy over this exercise. I got carried away and couldn't sleep, so I just kept repeating the exercise until I fell into a dead stupor, which got me nothing but frustrated and grumpy the next day.

To enhance this spell:

- Perform at midday.

- Perform on Sunday in the hour of Mercury to enhance communication on a business deal.

- Perform on Sunday in the hour of the sun.

- Perform at Midsummer at dawn, at noon, and then again at dusk.

- Perform when the moon is in Leo.

Herbs, oils, candles, incenses, and powders can enhance your magick. The following three magickal aids, Morgana's Prosperity Incense, Morgana's Prosperity Powder, and Morgana's Prosperity Oil, can be used anytime during the month and are excellent spell enhancers for any situation the universe sets before you.

Morgana's Prosperity Incense

Morgana owns a magickal shop called Morgana's Chamber in New York City's popular Manhattan district (her shop's address is 242 W. 10th Street, NY, NY, 10014). This petite Witch of the new millennium has a definite flair for cooking up powerful, magickal concoctions, which she has generously shared here.

Incense helps to put you in the right frame of magickal mind, acts as a psychic doorbell to Divinity that you are in need of assistance, and becomes part of the overall magickal working.

> **Supplies: One cup cedar shavings** (cedar has many magickal uses, including healing, purification, protection, and prosperity, and comes from a fragrant evergreen tree); **½ tablespoon benzoin resin** (benzoin resin—from the styrax tree cultivated in Java, Sumatra, and Thailand—is commonly used among magickal practitioners as a base for an incense mixture); **½ tablespoon dried cinquefoil** (a favorite of Pennsylvania Dutch Pow-Wow artists, used primarily for conjuring prosperity and healing); **one teaspoon High John the Conqueror Oil** (an all-around Southern favorite, this oil is associated with breaking hexes, prosperity, love, success, healing from depression, and happiness); **thirteen drops vetivert oil** (prosperity, love, and breaking hexes, a definite fast-cash oil and a favorite of Southern folk magickal practitioners); **nine drops orange oil** (love, luck, money, and divination).

> **Instructions:** Grind cedar shavings and benzoin resin together. Add cinquefoil and oils, mix well. Use anytime

in conjunction with your prosperity spells. This incense can be used on charcoal or match-lit. Store in a cool, dry area in an airtight container. Fire is the primary element of this magickal incense, and its zodiac associations are Leo, Aries, and Sagittarius. When using the zodiac energies, remember Aries is to start a project, Leo is to fix or hold firm or defend the project, and Sagittarius is to get things moving that may have stalled.

To enhance this mixture:

- Make on a new or full moon.

- Make when the moon is in Aries, Leo, or Sagittarius.

- Make on a Tuesday (for more aggressive, fiery pursuits).

- Make on Midsummer, when the sun is at its zenith.

- Make on a Thursday in the hour of Jupiter, Venus, or the sun.

- Make on Sunday in the hour of Jupiter, Venus, or the sun.

- Make on Friday in the hour of Jupiter, Venus, or the sun (especially if a partnership is involved).

Morgana's Prosperity Powder

The primary purpose of any magickal powder is to influence human thought and emotion, or to influence once-human unseen energies that have attached themselves to a particular person. This means that a magickal powder directly affects the behavior of people. Although some magickal individuals may argue that powders are an unethical form of magick, there are certain situations where powders can be useful and ethical. This particular blend combines the energies of success and protection, and therefore is not harmful in any way.

> **Supplies: One cup cedar shavings** (prosperity, protection, and purification); **one tablespoon pine needles** (prosperity, protection, healing, fertility, and purification); **one teaspoon cinnamon** (success, love, healing, prosperity, and spirituality); **one pinch dragon's blood herb** (increases the potency of any mixture); gold, silver, and green glitter.

> **Instructions:** Mix the first four ingredients together and grind into a fine powder. Add glitter and mix. Store in a

cool area in an airtight container. Use powder in spells or alone.

Note: Air is the primary element in any magickal powder, corresponding to the air signs of Aquarius, Gemini, and Libra. Libra starts a project, Aquarius fixes it in place, and Gemini changes.

To enhance this mixture:

- Make on the new or full moon.

- Make when the moon is in Libra, Gemini, or Aquarius.

- Make on Beltaine (May Day).

- Make when the wind is considerably active in your area, or when the wind is coming from the north.

- Make on a Wednesday in the hour of Venus.

- Make at dawn.

Use powder in the following manner:

- Scatter on the ground or carpet, particularly in a doorway, to attract customers, a raise, or a promotion.

- Scatter outside of a bank when you seek a loan.

- Load in candles for success and business protection spells (see page 185 for loading).

- Put in a cloth bag with a horse chestnut. Place in purse or pocket.

- Sprinkle on your money.

- Add a bit to your favorite money incense.

Morgana's Prosperity Oil

Supplies: One tonka bean (money, courage, and wishes); **three parts bergamot oil** (also called orange mint; for money and success, bergamot oil is derived from the rind of a fruit that grows in Italy); **two parts patchouli oil** (money, fertility, and lust; patchouli comes from India and Indonesia and became popular in Britain in the 1820s, where it was used to dye Indian shawls and added to India ink); **one part vetivert oil** (money, breaking hexes, and love); **one drop pineapple oil** (money, luck, and chastity); **sweet almond oil (base)** (money and wisdom).

Instructions: Put tonka bean in an interestingly shaped bottle. Fill half of the bottle with sweet almond oil. Add the other oils and mix well. Store in a cool, dry place. Use the oil to anoint money, candles, spell papers, etc. Oils fall under the influence of Scorpio, Pisces, or Cancer. Use Cancer to begin a project; Scorpio to "fix" or set in place; and Pisces to change a situation.

To enhance this mixture:

• Make on a new or full moon.

• Make during a rain shower.

• Make on Yule (December 21), Christmas, or Chanukah.

• Make at midnight.

• Make when the moon is in Scorpio (for intensity).

• Make on Sunday in the hour of the sun.

Use oils in the following manner:

• Anoint candles.

• Anoint physical objects.

- Add a bit to your favorite money incense.

- This oil is safe for self-anointing.

Pennsylvania Dutch Money Manifesting Powder

If you're into herbs and grinding stuff up, here's another money powder recipe. In Pow-Wow, the four ingredients listed below have an affinity for drawing money and health. Pow-Wow artists loved to use Three Lady Charms (or Three Angel Charms), which we'll employ here to keep the thread of authenticity between the herbs and the chant. The Three Lady Charms refer to the ancient worship of the Goddess in her aspect of triplicity; therefore, you could concentrate on any trinity you choose, or you may simply call them the Three Ladies.

Supplies: Five almonds, crushed to a fine powder; one part cinquefoil (five-finger grass); one part dried mint; one part orris root.

To give your powder extra oomph, you can also add a colored base powder often sold in magickal candle shops or three drops of your favorite money-drawing or herbal oil. **Tip:** If you are in a pinch, you can dry the herbs in your microwave. **Note:** You can use almond oil to anoint magickal tools and candles as an empowering agent for wealth, love, and success.

Instructions: On Sunday or Thursday, in the hour of Jupiter (long-term ventures) or Venus (short-term cash), crush the ingredients with a mortar and pestle (or in a blender). Say:

> **In the name of the elements of earth and air,**
> **bless this spell.**

Empower in the name of the Three Ladies, saying:

> **Three ladies came from the east, bringing health and wealth. The first said, "You need some." The second said, "We make some." The third said, "We give health and wealth to you. So mote it be!"**

Nordic triceps symbol

Repeat the chant three times. As you say the chant, sprinkle the powder on your doorstep, in your wallet or purse, or on a piece of paper describing a proposed project. Add to other spells in this book or to your own spells that I know you are going to design. Money powders, oils, and incenses are a very nice gesture on holidays, birthdays, or any day! (They are especially nice when a friend is down due to financial constraints.) Throw in a few green candles and you've created a gift to lift their spirits and share in their wish for prosperity. (Prosperity shared is prosperity gained.) Inscribe candles with the Nordic triceps symbol. If you affirm someone's right to be prosperous and happy, then you will gain prosperity and happiness in your own life, too.

To enhance this mixture:

- Make on the new or full moon.

- Make on Sunday in the hour of the sun or the hours of Jupiter or Venus.

- Make when the moon is in Aries, but empower when the moon is in Taurus.

- Make on New Year's Day.

- Make on Candlemas.

The Logical Spell
(If You Like Things a Bit More Complicated)

This one is strictly for the adept magickal worker. The supplies you will use depend entirely on what your spell is for, so you will need to sit down with a piece of paper and determine:

- Your overall goal.

- How many people are involved in the attainment of that goal.

- How many logical steps are needed to accomplish that goal.

- What sort of energy you want to work with: earth, air, water, fire, spirit, stellar, all of those listed, or a combination of those listed.

- An "out," in case you would wish to break the spell (which is a good idea for any type of spellcasting).

- Determine what color or colors would go with your goal. Match colors to each step, individual, or item in the process of attaining that goal (see color section in the appendices).

- Choose the correct moon phase and planetary hour to match the goal.

Supplies: A very long strip of rawhide; colored beads to match each step, individual, or item in the process of attaining that goal; one bead to represent your "out" (**Note:** you should be able to string the rawhide through the beads). There should be two beads of the same color representing your goal: one for the beginning, and one for the end.

Instructions: Visualize white light surrounding you and the supplies you plan to use. (Don't forget to have your piece of paper with you that lists all people, items, energies, steps, an "out," and the final goal.) Tie a knot at one end of the rawhide. State that this is the beginning. Slide the first goal bead next to the knot. Make another knot to secure this bead. The second bead (or successive beads, depending on how many you choose) will stand for the energies you wish to incorporate. For example, if you want to work with air energy, you might pick a yellow bead (fire—red; water—blue; earth—green; Spirit—silver; lunar—white; stellar—gold). Say the energy aloud. The next bead represents your first step. Repeat the step verbally as you add the bead. Add items, people, and successive steps, tying knots on each side of the bead to secure it. As you add each bead, say the goal aloud. The "out" bead goes next to last. The final bead is the goal bead (that matches the color of the first bead on the string).

At this stage, you have completed the string of beads. Take the string to each quarter (N, S, E, W) and ask for the blessings of that quarter. Ask for the blessings of Spirit. Hold the string out before you and touch each bead, indicating what that bead represents. (It is okay to use your paper if you have a complicated goal.) Do not break the rhythm of your cadence. Do not stop until you have reached the last goal bead. Thank the quarters and thank the energies you accessed. Work the string of beads as often as you like, repeating your list of items, energies, steps, and people until the goal has manifested. When you have received your desire, take the string back into your ritual circle, ask that the magick be dispersed, then cut the rawhide. Burn the rawhide. Save the beads for another spell.

Note: You can also make a "general" string of beads, like the angel rosary in my book *Angels: Companions in Magick*.[3] Years ago I designed a Birthday Spell on the same principle (printed in Llewellyn's 1995 *Magical Almanac*). In that spell, each bead stood for a year of one's life. For smaller goals (without many steps), you can use yarn and elbow macaroni, which is also a great way to teach kids spellwork.

To enhance this spell:

- Perform on your birthday.

- Perform on a new moon.

- Perform on January 1.

- Perform on May Day (Beltaine).

- Perform when the moon is in Aries.

----

3. Llewellyn, 1997.

The Manifestation Stone

This exercise works much like the golden cord spell, only this employs the use of a simple, smooth stone to manifest your desires. In studying Pennsylvania Dutch folk magick, I learned that plain stones have marvelous, potent energy—we just have to realize, accept, and learn to work with that energy.

Instructions: Go on a little trip to find a nice, smooth stone that fits in the palm of your hand (not too big— about the size of the heel of your thumb). If someone has recently given you a smooth stone (which is highly possible) this stone is probably your manifestation stone given to you from the universe through a friend. Wash the stone with spring water. Energize the stone in the name of your favorite (or patron) deity and claim this stone for manifestation work.

Sit quietly and begin rolling the stone in the palm of your hand (or from hand to hand). Close your eyes and take three deep breaths. Relax. Continue to roll the stone. Repeat in your mind, "This is my stone of mani-festation," until you get a little bored or sleepy. Then say:

I manifest _____

(stating what it is that you want to bring to yourself).

You can choose a goal, a way of life, a personal quality, an item—it doesn't matter. Keep repeating what you want to manifest while you roll the stone in your hands. Picture what it is that you want to manifest. When you feel a surge of energy or a slight tingling, it is time to stop for today. Repeat the exercise every day until you manifest your desire. Don't fret over what you want. If after twenty-eight days you have not manifested what you wanted, energize the stone again and repeat the exercise. Once you have manifested your goal, wash the stone again and pick a new goal. As with the golden cord exercise, keep practicing with your stone. Your stone will gain power over successive use, and you will gain confidence.

Note: If you have more than one goal that you want to work for simultaneously, you can use more than one stone, if that feels right to you. For example, I might work for a small goal in the morning and a larger goal

Norse money charm

at night, using two different stones. However, you can use the same stone for different goals. Stones do not seem to be meticulous. They do like to work.

To enhance this spell:

- Paint the money charm symbol (above) on the stone. This is a Norse symbol meaning "My need is great."

- Perform when the moon is in Virgo.

- Perform on a Wednesday in the hour of Mercury (if the spell involves the support of many people).

- Perform on Friday in the hour of the sun, Jupiter, or Mercury, depending on the energies you wish to manifest.

Prosperity Scroll

I love petition magick because of its simplicity. Here, we use the Celtic goddess Rosemerta for deity association. She is another cornucopia deity of harvest and a patroness of merchants and wealth. She's also been linked with the Roman-Celtic Mercury (though this is a stretch). Her Gaulish/British name means "good purveyor" and she is sometimes portrayed with a butter churn, but usually seen with the cornucopia.

Supplies: One-inch wide strip of parchment paper that is three feet long; a green-inked pen; your favorite incense.

Instructions: Draw the astrological sign of Taurus at the top of the strip ($\forall$). Write on the paper: ***"Holy Mother, manifest what I place upon this list."*** Make a list of what you desire on the paper (you will have a lot of extra space—that's okay). Roll the paper tightly into a little scroll. Pass the list over the incense, repeating the above charm nine times. Place the scroll in your purse, wallet, on your altar, by your desk, etc.—wherever you can add to it when you desire or hold it in your hand and repeat the charm when you feel like it. When the paper is full and you have received all that you asked for, thank Rosemerta, burn the paper, and begin a new list.

To enhance this spell:

• Perform at Lammas or when the moon is in Capricorn if the items you listed are those that you've worked on and you are ready to reap your harvest.

• Perform when a project is lagging and needs an extra boost when the moon is in Aries.

• Perform during the new or full moon.

Quick Spell idea: With Rosemerta's association to the butter churn, you can take an empty butter box, place your requests inside, sprinkle with your money powder and burn in an outside ritual fire as an offering to her.

House Wealth Incense

The primary deity for this recipe is Dagda (Daghdha), an Irish deity considered to be one of the two greatest kings of the Tuatha De Danann. He is an all-father deity, a military leader, and master tradesman who can invoke the seasons and who holds a cauldron of plenty called the Undry that could feed the whole earth. Dagda is sometimes called the Lord of Great Knowledge because he possesses all the knowledge of the universe. Not to be trifled with, he carries an enormous club that can bash an enemy's brains with a single blow. Dagda is not a white-light-and-bubbles kind of guy. He is portrayed as holding a large club or fork, symbolizing his control over the food supply of the cosmos.

> **Note:** Call on Dagda if you need money for food, your garden, or other aspect linked to your physical survival. He is also wonderful if you are having trouble on the job.
>
> As in the money powder, the ingredients of the house wealth incense each have magickal properties of their own.

Supplies: Three parts frankincense (linked both to solar [Apollo, Adonis, Ra] and lunar deities [Demeter], frankincense has been used in religious ceremonies for centuries as an herb of wealth and purification); **one part myrrh** (sacred to Aphrodite and Adonis [as well as Cybele, Hecate, Rhea, and Juno], this herb also has connections to the legend of the phoenix and the magickal aspects of rebirth); **one part patchouli** (usually a prime ingredient in wealth or love spells because of its ability to attract energies, people, or things); ½ **part allspice** (used for money, luck, and healing, and a great additive in Yule cookies, to bring prosperity into the home); ½ **part nutmeg** (another flexible herb used in money, wealth, health, and fidelity spells); ½ **part ginger** (love, money, success, strength, and power are the essential energies linked to this herb); **one pinch of household dust** (added to create sympathy between the herbal mixture and the place where you live); a charcoal incense brick; a blue candle; a purple candle.

Instructions: On Thursday, in the hour of the sun (or at midday), mix the ingredients. Grind with mortar and pestle (you can even use a blender, just remember to wash the bowl well when you're done). You can empower in the name of Dagda, your patron deity, a deity associated with prosperity (of which we've named several so far), or simply empower in the name of Spirit. Primary elements for this spell are earth (the herbs), air (the smoke), and fire (the charcoal). Burn on a charcoal brick before a mirror empowered for household protection and monetary success,[4] or carry around the entire house, fumigating all corners (including attic and basement). Empower the purple and blue candles for wealth and spiritual success. Allow these candles to completely burn. You can also sprinkle the incense on your hearthstone or on logs in your fireplace before the first fall burn, or last spring burn.

If times have been particularly bad, burn a black candle to dispel negativity.

To enhance this mixture:

• Make over the Yule, Christmas, and Chanukah holiday season (great for gifts).

------

4. *The Magical Household* by Scott Cunningham and David Harrington. Llewellyn, 1997. Page 165.

- Make on the new, waxing, or full moon.

- Make for that special friend who just bought a house.

- Make for spring and fall housecleaning.

- Make when the moon is in Virgo, then empower when the moon is in Taurus.

- Make on a Sunday for success or Monday or Friday for those correspondences associated with the home.

Prosperity Floor Wash

Folk superstitions from various cultures believe that the floors and corners of your home trap negativity, especially if coated with ground-in dirt, which impedes the health and prosperity of the family unit. Many occult shops and botanicals carry pre-pared floor washes that are to be used on a clean, dry floor, doorknobs, or store counters to improve the prosperity of the home or establishment.

Supplies: One bucket; one handful of salt; three cinnamon sticks; three drops honey; one teaspoon cinquefoil; one teaspoon powdered eggshell; a handful of violets, roses, or lavender; one sliced lemon; one new wooden spoon; a mop; sage (comes in a smudge stick or loose); a fireproof pot.

Instructions: Wash all wooden or tile floors with a good detergent. Allow to dry. In a bucket, mix the salt, cinnamon sticks, honey, cinquefoil, powdered eggshell, and flowers. Squeeze in lemon juice and two gallons water. Mix three times with a new wooden spoon. Mop the floor with the mixture. Allow to dry. Sweep herbs and flowers out the door. Light the sage in the fireproof pot and brush the fragrant smoke in swirling motions in the corners of the room.

To enhance this mixture:

- When choosing a day or time to make your floor wash and implement the energies, keep in mind that Jupiter energy lends itself to the big picture and Venus energy manifests in fast cash.

- Make during a new or waxing moon.

- Use before and after a large social or family event.

- Use in your place of business.

- Sprinkle in your vehicle.

The Magickal Check

To do this spell, you will need to use one of the checks from your checking account. Write yourself a magickal check in green ink for services rendered to yourself. Do not date the check. The fee should directly relate to a specific goal, which you will write on the bottom, left-hand corner of the check. For example, you might write: *For writing a popular fiction.* (That's what I wrote.) You may have a goal of $250 or $50,000, it doesn't matter. Sprinkle the check with cinnamon. Seal the back by using the equal-armed cross (page 56) and money oil. This is your special, magickal check. You can put it in your wallet or purse, or in a magick box or jar. Then, each paycheck, write a smaller check to yourself for services rendered. It doesn't have to be much—$5 will work just as well as $50. The act of pay-ing yourself is a psychological booster that helps to affirm that yes, you *can* pay yourself; yes, you *can* reach your goals, and yes, you *do* deserve to be paid! Be sure that you actually spend the money on yourself. No coughing it up to the kids, spouse, friends, sister, or in-laws. This belongs to you. Actor Jim Car-rey wrote a check to himself for $50,000 long before he became famous. And you know—he got to cash that check! (And no, he didn't get the idea from me. It was his own.)

To enhance this spell:

- If the check represents prosperity from your hard work, business venture, or banking expertise, then write while the moon is in Capricorn.

- Write on a new or waxing moon.

- Surround the check with a gold candle, a green candle, and a red candle (for action); light the candles for seven days, from the new through the waxing moon (only burn for the whole time if candles are in a fire-safe area and there are no children or pets nearby).

Wheel of Fortune

Although deceptively simple, this is one of my favorite spells of manifestation, and is considered an "oldie but goodie" among magickal folk.[5] We're going to work again with Juno (or Fortuna), as both goddesses are historically linked to the wheel of fortune. Why reinvent the wheel? Er, goddess. Whatever.

For this spell we are going to use the runes Feoh ($\mathtext{Y}$) or Gyfu (✕) (especially if you require something that will be in partnership with another, such as a business proposition).

Supplies: One piece of white paper; colored pencils; green marker; a list of your desires; blessed spring water; one green candle.

Instructions: On the full or waxing moon, sit down at a table with your supplies. Hold the green candle in your hands, and say:

O creature of earth, assist me to magnify my desires.

---

5. Based on a spell from *Practical Color Magick* by Raymond Buckland. Llewellyn, 1983.

Light the candle, and say:

O creature of fire, assist me to magnify my desires.

Draw a large circle on your paper with the green marker. This circle represents the magick circle. Divide your circle into pie slices, one slice for each desire. On each slice, in green marker, write your desire. With the colored pencils, draw an image that corresponds to your desire in each pie slice. For example, recently I found one of my old color wheels tucked under my altar stone. Two years ago, I asked for the following: a new computer that would meet my writing needs; a new refrigerator; new beds for the kids; a good car that would meet my transportation needs, be in excellent condition, and be safe; the smooth publication of one of my books; the opportunity to promote my books. As I looked over my list, I realized that I had received everything I had asked for, and more.

On your paper, draw any runes or other magickal sigils that you feel appropriate, or the runes suggested above. Write "In the name of Juno" on the back of the paper.

Sprinkle with a bit of blessed spring water, and say:

O creature of water, grant my will with my desire.

Blow three times on the paper, and say:

O creature of air, grant my will with my desire.

Then say:

**My desires become manifest in Juno's name.
So mote it be!**

Seal with an equal-armed cross (page 56).

When you have finished the color wheel, envision yourself surrounded by white light. Present the color wheel to the quarter energies (N, S, E, W), asking for blessings on your desires. Invoke your chosen deity (in our example we are using Juno), again asking for blessings. Thank the quarters. Thank deity. Put your color wheel in a safe place. I normally hide my color wheels so that when I do find them a few years down the road, I can smile at the affirmation of what I have accomplished. When you do discover where you've hidden that color wheel, thank the quarters and deity again, then burn the paper.

Should most things be granted, yet one item remains unmanifest (and provided that you still want the item), do not burn the old color wheel. Instead, create a new color wheel and glue it on top of the old one to hold on to the continuity of the previous magick.

To enhance this spell:

- Turn your wheel into a star—even better, superimpose the star over the wheel. Use the points of the star for more spiritual pursuits.

- Perform on New Year's Day.

- Change the wheel into its opposite, citing all the things you want to banish from your life. Perform this type of spell on a Saturday in the hour of Saturn, on the dark of the moon, or on a waning moon.

Manifesting Harmony with Others: The Enchanted God Bowl

If you are a merchant of any kind or involved with travel, communications, or big business, this is the spell for you. A little while back I was having trouble with a particular business organization, especially in the area of communication. It wasn't that I was doing anything wrong and it wasn't that the people in the organization were bad—we simply weren't communicating properly, and I knew it. I tried all the regular channels of communication first, but I just didn't seem to be getting anywhere. This difficulty was affecting my prosperity, and therefore I knew I had to do something about the situation. (Never call something a problem, always called it a "situation." One of my old bosses taught me that one, and he was right. How you perceive events has a lot to do with how you succeed—or don't—within that event.) Anyway, it was time to wiggle those magickal fingers of mine!

There were a lot of things I could have done. That's the nice thing about magick—you have a whole compendium of choices—but I wanted to do something special, something just for this particular prob . . . er, situation. To that end, I designed an enchanted god bowl out of clay and dedicated it to Mercury (Roman god of communications, whose Greek counterpart is Hermes) on a Wednesday during a new moon. Mercury was also the protector of the corn trade in Sicily, which gives us a good correspondence if we wish to protect what we already own, as well as enhance our trading power. The merchant's guild was known as Mercuriales. Mercury's yearly festival fell on May 15 and merchants would sprinkle themselves and their goods with corn meal as a gift and sacrifice to prosperity, followed by a good dousing of holy water.

It took me all day to make the bowl, and as I worked the clay I kept my thoughts focused on improving communications between myself and the organization. I thought of the feast of Mercury, what it would have been like, and kept the energies of Mercury in mind. The element of mercury is called quicksilver. Mercury's attributes include the winged hat, winged shoes, and the caduceus (double snakes on a stick, signifying the healing arts). The astrological symbol for Mercury is ☿.

That night I wrote down exactly what I wanted to happen:
Clear and loving communication between myself and any
employee of that business that would lead to mutual success.
I placed the bowl on my altar, then placed the paper in the
bowl, repeating my desire.

Within twenty-four hours, a flurry of communication
ensued and the situation was resolved. Since I worked with this
business often, I kept the bowl strictly for communicating with
any employee of that establishment. Every time I wanted to
work with them, I simply put my request in the bowl. When
my request was granted, I burned the paper and thanked deity.
When I completed my business with that company, I broke
the bowl in ritual and returned the clay to the earth.

To enhance this spell:

- Make the bowl on a Wednesday in the hour of Mercury.

- Surround the bowl with brown and gold candles.
  Burn for friendship in monetary pursuits.

- Combine the symbol for Mercury (☿) and the Sun (☉).
  Inscribe on the bowl and on the candles.

Egg and Brown Sugar Spell

From Russian sorcery to Pennsylvania Dutch folk magick, the egg has been a prominent ingredient in many magickal operations. Seen as the manifestation of new life, in Germany eggs were often plowed into the fields in autumn to ensure a plentiful harvest for the following year. The egg is also considered an appropriate sacrifice to the dead in Asia and Europe, and can be used when requesting magickal assistance from those beyond the veil.

Cinquefoil, commonly known as five-finger grass, figures prominently in Pennsylvania Dutch magickal practices. Seen as "a helping hand," the herb has a variety of uses, from protection to securing wealth. This herb can also be brewed and cooled, then used to cleanse magickal tools, sprinkled in the corner of any room to dispel negativity, or employed as anointing water.

Supplies: One part brown sugar; one part cinquefoil;

one part patchouli herb and incense; mortar and pestle; one brown egg; one brown marker; one brown candle; almond oil. Our color scheme of brown is to promote harmony and feelings of kinship with the universe.

Instructions: Mix the brown sugar, cinquefoil, and patchouli herb together with mortar and pestle. On a full moon, write what you need most on the brown egg with the brown marker. You can list several desires on one egg. In a ritual circle, light the incense. Rub almond oil on your brown candle. Hold the candle in your hand and concentrate on the desires you wrote on the egg. Light the candle. Hold the egg in your hand and name your desires aloud, saying **"I draw forth"** before each desire. For example: "I draw forth positive abundance. I draw forth a purse with many pockets. I draw forth a new refrigerator. I draw forth harmony. I draw forth a small, pink, stuffed elephant." (Gotcha!) Ask for blessings from a chosen deity. Pass the egg through the incense, stating your goals once again. Pass the egg through the candle flame, repeating your desires. As the candle burns, bury the egg on your property. (If you don't have land, use a small container with potting soil, but place the container outdoors because as the egg rots, it may smell up your living space.) Dig a small hole in the ground and add the brown sugar. Place the egg on top. As you bury the egg, say:

**I give blessings and love to the universe.
I manifest positive Spirit into myself. As this egg rots,
my desires will manifest. And it is so.**

Let the candle burn to completion. As the egg is a good gift for the dead, you can speak to a specific ancestor when formulating your desires and then again when burying the egg. If you do this, sprinkle a little patchouli on top of the ground over the buried egg (as patchouli also relates to honoring the dead).

To enhance this spell:

- Perform on August 1 (Lammas) or on the day that you remove the last of the harvest from your garden.

- Perform under the Harvest Moon.

- Perform on Oestre or Easter—as eggs relate to spring, you may wish to use this spell in any spring ritual.

Egg Prosperity Charm

This spell is a bit more complicated, takes a little dexterity on your part, and will be time-consuming but well worth the struggle.

Supplies: One egg at room temperature; darning needle or X-Acto knife; a cork; green egg dye; ⅛ teaspoon each mint, cinquefoil, and cinnamon; a small cutting of your hair; a small piece of loadstone, magnetized iron fillings, or a small holey stone; a silver charm of your choice (keep your choices tiny); three drops money oil.

Instructions: Insert the eye of the darning needle into the cork. Holding the cork end, puncture the egg on the top and the bottom by rotating the needle and applying light pressure. (It may take you a few eggs to get the hang of this, so you might want to set out more than one to reach room temperature.) Make the hole at the narrow end large enough that your collected ingredients will fit through the hole. Blow out the contents of the egg through the holes that you made from the wide bottom to alleviate strain on the narrow top. As the contents of the egg begin to dribble, shake the egg up and down to hasten the flow. After you have emptied the egg, you are ready to dye the shell. After dying, dry the shell in the sun. In a prosperity ceremony written by yourself, add the herbs and other small objects. Empower the entire egg for general prosperity. Add the money oil. Place on your altar or in some other safe place in your home. Renew once a year.

To enhance this spell:

- Employ this spell on Beltaine or New Year's Day.

- Add the astrological symbols of Taurus for long-term luxury energy; Gemini for a quick change of luck; Aries if during a time when you need an extra boost; or Scorpio for intensity (see appendix).

To Win a Court Case That Involves Receiving Money

This spell only works if you are to fairly receive money from a court case.

Supplies: One blue candle (for peace in your prosperity);
one red candle (for fast action); one cake of blue soap;
the names of all who will reside in judgement over you
in the court case, including the names of those who are
going against you; one glass of water; a small amount of
lemon oil.

Instructions: If you can, begin this spell seven days before
going to court. Carve the names of the people listed
above on the bar of soap. Place the soap in the glass of
water. Light the red and blue candles, asking for
a fair judgement. Invoke the four archangels—
Michael, Raphael, Gabriel, and Uriel—asking
for their protection and persuasion in the court
case. Allow the candles to burn completely.
When the court case is over, dispose of the water
and soap in an environmentally safe way.

Rub the lemon oil on your hands and the
soles of your shoes before you go into court.

To enhance this spell:

- Talk to your guardian angel before you go into court and keep talking to your guardian angel while you are in court.

- Ask the angels of justice to help you as you enter the courthouse.

Roll of the Dice

Did you ever get the feeling that what you are about to do with your money or a job you are trying to get may surely be by chance alone? This spell is to help you increase your odds of success in any endeavor.

Supplies: Two dice; money oil; one lodestone (you can substitute a magnet); one red flannel bag; one red candle; one piece of paper.

Instructions: Write exactly what you want on the piece of paper. Anoint the candle with the money oil (or other type of attraction oil). Light the candle, asking for assistance from Spirit in this unknown venture. Anoint the dice in the same manner, asking for assistance. Empower the lodestone to bring good fortune to you. Roll and throw the dice seven times, each time asking that the odds for you be strengthened and the odds against you be lessened. Place the dice, the piece of paper, and the lodestone in the red bag. Allow the candle to burn completely. Carry the bag with you. You can take out the dice and roll anytime, repeating your request. Re-empower the bag every full moon (even if you did not make the original bag on the full moon).

Helping Your Bank Account and Other Investments Grow

Children really enjoy helping you with this spell. It's an easy way to teach them creative visualization and help your bank account sprout lots of dollar bills. The astrological sign of Capricorn rules money and banking. Put the symbol of Capricorn (♑) at the top of your chart.

Supplies: One poster board; colored pencils or markers; your recent bank statement; green construction paper; glue.

Instructions: Find your recent bank or investment statement. Write the account number on the back of the poster board. Draw a circle around the number to protect the investments you already have. On the front of the poster board draw a large tree with lots and lots of branches. At the top of the tree write your monetary goal. At the bottom of the tree write your current balance. Cut out three hundred and sixty-five leaves. (You can make them little leaves or, if the idea of cutting all those leaves gives you heart failure, you can use play money or leaf stickers.) Hold your hands over the leaves and the poster board, and say:

Each day I add a leaf, each day my balance grows.
Each day I add a leaf, until I reach my goal.
With harm to none, so mote it be!

Hang the poster board in a prominent place. Each day, glue a leaf on your tree, visualizing your bank accounts growing to reach your goal. Repeat the spell as you hang the leaf. When you have reached your goal, or three hundred and sixty-five days are up, burn the poster board. Start a new one with the old goal (if you are still working toward that goal) or set yourself a new goal.

To enhance this spell:

• Construct two weeks after school begins (the first week or so is just too busy; by week three, things settle down enough for you to introduce this project to your kids).

Prosperity Gourd

This spell requires you to think ahead a bit and collect some nice gourds during the harvest season. If you have a green thumb you may wish to plant some gourds in your garden over the summer months. We put up a trellis because we didn't have enough room with our raised beds, and then we lost the seeds so I had to plant cucumbers. (I guess the Goddess wanted bread and butter pickles that year.) I had to buy my gourds at the grocery store. Over the winter months, dry the gourds in your attic, basement, or garage—anywhere that is cool and dry. Gourds will occasionally get bad spots on them while drying, but they are still good so don't throw them away.

Supplies: One dried gourd; thin wire or string; one part dragon's blood herb; one part mustard seed; one part sage; one part cinquefoil; five new pennies; five kernels dried corn.

Instructions: Cut off the top of the gourd with a sharp knife. Punch a hole half an inch from the top of the opening on each side of the gourd. Thread the wire into the holes, allowing a loop for hanging. Secure the wire by twisting it. On the full moon, mix the dragon's blood herb, mustard seed, and cinquefoil together. Empower for protection of your finances and future bounty. Place in the gourd. Add the five new pennies and the five kernels of dried corn. Hold your hands over the gourd, pray, and state your desire for future plentiful, positive harvests and protection for what you already have. Under the full moon, hang the gourd outside of your front door.

If you want to be decorative, you can paint the outside of the gourd with green or blue paint and add your favorite magickal sigils for prosperity.

To enhance this spell:

- Make during the full or new moon.

- Make during your Lammas, Fall Equinox, or Samhain celebration.

Simple Potpourri Prosperity Shell

The primary deity for this easy spell is the Yoruban Oshun, goddess of the sweet waters. As we've seen with various goddesses, Oshun has many names and many faces. As Oshun Ana (*ana* meaning first goddess), she is the goddess of luxury and love. The original legend around this deity indicates that she was birthed in the headwaters of the Oshun River, hence her association with the sweet waters of rivers, streams, creeks, and wells. She is said to cure the sick and impart fertility with her loving essence. As Oshun Telargo, Oshun is seen as the modest one, and as Oshun Yeye Moro, she is a formidable seductress. Her male counterpart is Chango (Shango), god of thunder (sometimes she is seen as his sister or mistress). African gods and goddesses are different, as they require gifts if you wish the blessings of their favor. Oshun loves pumpkins, sweets, gold, yellow roses, yellow candles, and pretty things in general; however, once you give something to Oshun, you cannot take it back. The item belongs to her forever, and she is known to curse those who renege on their promises or take gifts back from her. Devotees of Oshun wear amber beads. If you have a piece of amber and can part with it, then this is a wonderful gift for this goddess. The day of Oshun is Friday under the planet of Venus.

Note: African deities are fussy. They will either work with you, or they won't. Much like the Celtic Morrigan, African deities pick you—you do not have the luxury of choosing them. Other gods and goddesses you can choose for this spell are Juno (Roman); Rosemerta (Celtic); or Dagda (Celtic).

Supplies: Four ounces rose buds; ¼ ounce tonka beans; ¼ ounce cinnamon; two ounces powdered orris root; ¼ ounce dried mint; ¼ ounce dried orange peel; two glass bowls (do not use metal, or your fragrance will be spoiled); a wooden spoon; large glass jar with cork stopper or glass top; ten drops money oil; one large seashell.

Instructions: Crush tonka beans. In the large bowl, combine the tonka beans, cinnamon, orris root, and mint (the orris root is the fixative; without this herb, your potpourri would quickly lose its fragrance). In the other bowl, lightly crush the rose buds. Mix all ingredients together lightly with the wooden spoon. Add the money oil to the dry ingredients and stir again in a clockwise direction, visualizing prosperity coming into your home or place of business. Transfer the mixture into the glass jar and cover. Allow the mixture to settle for two weeks in a cool, dark place. Shake every other day. When you feel the mixture has sufficiently aged, pour into the seashell and place on an altar dedicated to Oshun. Save the remainder of the mixture for your prosperity poppet or charm bag.

To enhance this spell:

- Leave an offering to Oshun beside sweet water.

- Mix on Midsummer's Day.

- Mix on the full or waxing moon.

- If you desperately need money, you can place five yellow roses in a gallon of water, then burn a yellow candle, asking Oshun to bring you money as quickly as possible. Don't forget your offering.

Prosperity Poppet

Poppets are cloth, clay, or wax effigies that work through sympathetic magick[6] and can be used for a variety of magickal intent. Poppets may be one of the oldest feminine magickal applications, birthed from Middle Eastern motherhood charms, made from clay and menstrual blood, designed to protect children. Poppets also served as surrogate sacrifices in several areas under Celtic influence. The idea was to give back to the Mother what She gave to Her people in the form

----

6. Those things that share energy, similarity, or likeness.

of a corn dolly, scarecrow, or wicker effigy. Most poppet magick includes adding something that belongs to the person the poppet represents, such as hair, nail clippings, blood, earth from a footprint, or a piece of favored clothing. Here, you will be making a poppet that represents yourself, and you will be working for personal prosperity.

Supplies: Two squares green felt; red thread; one piece of lightweight cardboard; a pencil; a small picture of yourself; a lock of your hair or nail clippings; a black marker; four foreign coins.

Instructions: Make a simple drawing on the cardboard that looks like a gingerbread man or woman. This is you and the drawing will be your pattern for cutting the two pieces of felt. Cut out the pattern and lay it on the two pieces of felt and cut out the figure. Use the red thread to stitch up three-fourths of the poppet. The red will activate the green prosperity energy of the poppet. Leave a large enough hole to easily stuff the poppet. Place the picture of yourself, the herbs, and the lock of hair in the poppet. Place a coin in each arm and each leg. Sew shut.

Hold your hands over the poppet to draw prosperity and positive abundance toward you, asking for the blessings of divinity. Hang in a safe place. Renew the herbs every six months.

To enhance this spell:

- Surround poppet with red candles for lots of action.

- Make poppets as a group project, then attach to a belt. Dance the spiral dance at Midsummer.

- Make when the moon is in Taurus to fix and hold luxury.

- Make on the new or waxing moon.

Prosperity Charm or Conjuring Bag

The prosperity charm or conjuring bag works the same as the prosperity poppet, with one vital difference: the color of the bag should be red and the thread green. You can make the bag with a drawstring so that changing the herbs every six months will be an easier task. Remember to add your picture and a lodestone to magnify the manifestation. You might also wish to add a piece of St. John's Wort to protect your future riches. For fast cash, empower in the hour of Venus. For long-term expansion, empower in the hour of Jupiter. Carry the bag in your pocket, purse, or briefcase.

To Get a Bank Loan

This spell is to be used for any transaction where you wish to receive money from a bank (the legal way, of course).

> **Supplies:** One small bowl of water; five yellow floating candles; one yellow rose; five mint leaves; piece of paper with bank's name on it; change for a dollar.

> **Instructions:** Before you fill out the loan application, go to the bank and receive change for one dollar. You will use this change for the spell. On the day that you sign the loan application, begin the spell. Set the bowl on top of the name of the bank. Place the coins from the change you got at the bank in the bottom of the bowl. Add the five mint leaves to the water. Place the rose on top. At

noon, light one of the floating candles and place in the bowl. Concentrate on the bank giving you the loan with the best interest possible. Invoke your guardian angel for help. Let the candle burn. Each day for the next four consecutive days, place another lit candle in the bowl at noon and invoke your guardian angel. Do not remove the candles that are no longer burning. After you have received the loan, thank your guardian angel. Keep any candle remnants in case you have trouble paying the loan later on, as they psychically connect you to the loan. You also may wish to work with the candle remnants to help you pay your bill on time or to banish your overall debt.

To enhance this spell:

- Do not sign paperwork or apply for a loan when the moon is void of course or when Mercury is retrograde.

- Moon in first and second quarters favors the lender, in third and fourth quarters favors the borrower.

Spell for Business Success

If you own your own business or are self-employed in some other way, here's a great spell to give your new or old business a boost.

Supplies: One large dinner plate; ¼ cup corn meal; seven foreign coins; one small red flannel bag; your choice of prosperity incense; your choice of money oil (if you don't have money oil, use olive or almond oil); one green candle; one yellow candle; one red candle; one blue candle; one lodestone (can substitute a magnet). Write the name of your business (or what the business venture is all about) on a piece of paper. Carve the symbol of the sun (☉) on each candle.

Instructions: Anoint each candle with oil. Put the name of your business underneath the plate. Sprinkle the plate with the corn meal, asking for blessings from the goddess of all harvests. Arrange the seven foreign coins on the bed of corn meal in the shape of a cross, four coins across, four coins down. Set the green candle at the top of the arrangement, the yellow candle to the right, the red candle at the bottom, and the blue candle at the left of the arrangement. Put the lodestone directly in the center of your coin pattern. Light the candles, beginning with the green candle, asking the goddess of all harvests to bring you business success. Light the incense, repeating your request. Allow the candles and incense to burn completely. Place the coins, the lodestone, and the corn meal in the red bag. Carry the red bag with you as much as possible, or place somewhere in your business. Renew this spell every six months or when you feel the need.

Freebies and Risks

That's right: there are no freebies. *Ever.* There must always be an equal exchange of energy between yourself and another, regardless of the event, situation, or need. If there is not an equal exchange, then you will eventually suffer. Does this mean that you can't be charitable? Not at all. I said "equal exchange of energy," not necessarily a monetary fee for your services. Many of us were brought up with the idea that charity is the highest form of giving—which is true on its spiritual level. What becomes disturbing is the behavior of many individuals who feel that they should receive something for nothing simply because they breathe. When trying to get your finances on track, don't be so generous that you overextend yourself or leave yourself open to various scams that milk you of your paycheck. If something looks too good to be true, then it probably *is* too good to be true. Use a divination tool, consult outside sources that have knowledge of an individual, corporation, or financial institution, and talk to your guardian angel before you take any sort of risk with your money. Finally, Shakespeare's adage of "neither a borrower nor lender be" should become your magickal mantra in as many of your financial dealings as possible. My adage is "never borrow money from a friend and never lend your friends money." If you want to make a gift to someone, that's different, but owing friends or having friends owe you gets tied up with all sorts of nasty emotional issues. Don't bother to go there.

Quickies for Manifesting Prosperity

Performing spells, ceremonies, and exercises to improve your prosperity are fantastic when you have the time. What do you do when you've been faithfully working that manifesting or banishing magick and now you've got a trip to go on, a bus to catch, a date to meet, or homework to do? Sometimes there just aren't enough hours in the day. Here are some magickal quickies to keep your confidence up and prosperity flowing freely through your life. Quickies do not take the place of your regular magickal work, but are helpful to keep things moving at a steady pace.

- Place dried seaweed under the rug in the busiest portion of the house to draw luck and prosperity to you.

- Wash your windows with ammonia and vinegar to bring the blessings of the wind.

- Buy a regulator clock (or other chiming time mechanism). As the chimes sound on the hour, repeat your favorite prosperity affirmation.

- Position furniture or other decorative objects in the corners of your room to keep the energy flowing smoothly.

- Paint the inside of your bathroom door black, and keep it closed at all times to keep your prosperity from flushing out of the house.

- Use a holey stone (stones with natural holes, found at the seashore or in a creek bed) to pull positive energy toward you.

- Sprinkle cinquefoil in the bottom of your wallet, purse, safe, money box, and so on to give you that helping hand in the prosperity department.

- Blow bubbles with a straw in your morning coffee to bring about a prosperous day (I'm not kidding).

- To draw a particular item toward you, draw a pentacle on a piece of paper. Take a toy image of what you desire and paint your name on the underside of the image. Place the object in the center of the pentacle. Leave untouched until you receive what you desire. Surround with a circle of salt for extra protection of your desire.

- To change your luck, add one tablespoon of nutmeg to six cups of boiling water. Steep for three hours. Use for body anointing or add to a ritual bath. If you have a sensitivity to unusual things in the bath water (I do), then you can use as a rinse while you are in the shower.

- Empower gold glitter and sprinkle on your doorstep to bring prosperity into the home.

- Buy an easy book on feng shui (the Chinese art of placement) and mix with your prosperity magick.

- Begin new ventures during the increase of the moon.

- Sign important papers, contracts, or agreements when the moon is increasing.

Quickies for the Business Owner

- Wrap three foreign coins in gold cloth. Place in the cash register.

- Stick a clove of garlic with nine pins and hang close to the front door.

- Rubber band a large bill around an empowered mandrake root. Place in cash register.

- Stuff a poppet with three dollar bills and three foreign coins. Hide under the counter by the register.

- Cleanse your store, vending area, or desk every day with blessed spring water or sage. Be sure to use the floor wash to encourage a constant flow of customers.

- From a regular card deck, take the ace, ten, nine, and seven of diamonds. Anoint with prosperity oil (page 84) and place together in your purse or pocket. Renew once a month on the full moon.

- Soak a clove of garlic in your favorite magickal money drawing oil. Hang directly under the cash register or the desk where you work.

Learn to Go with Your Gut

Throughout this book I give you lots of information on deities, herbs, candle colors, phases of the moon, planetary energies, etc. Be willing to experiment with these correspondences. The moon in the various signs is a subjective type of magick, and may not work for everyone the same way. Learn to go with your gut feelings on any issue. For example, everything may be perking along fine, you're working with the new and waxing moons, it's a money-in day or week, and suddenly you feel like banishing negative energies, but it isn't

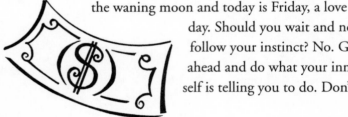

the waning moon and today is Friday, a love day. Should you wait and not follow your instinct? No. Go ahead and do what your inner self is telling you to do. Don't get all tied up over why you feel this way or that way. Go ahead and anoint the black candle. Roll the black candle in red glitter. Burn the candle and ask Spirit (or your chosen deity) to dissipate any negative energies around you.

Now it's time for you to take a peek at what I developed in the realm of banishing poverty (if you haven't already) and learn how to turn that waning moon energy into financial success!

4

Banishing Poverty

In the last two chapters we worked on manifesting. In this section we're going to work on pushing negative energies away from you as well as taking a good look at your current financial state and how you can work with even the messiest monetary problem in a positive way. According to Debtor's Anonymous,[1] twenty million Americans are overwhelmed by debt at this very moment. In all, it is thought that over eighty percent of the American population experiences some sort of financial difficulty—including many who would never admit it to their friends and family, let alone a survey.

They say that you teach best what you most need to learn, and this little adage has proven itself numerous times in my life. The spells in this chapter are my gift to you, designed and tested by me over a very rough time in my life. I know they work. You can best believe that I toiled over every correspondence, every moon phase, and every supply used for each spell until I felt the techniques were perfect. I called or traveled to people who had decades of training in one magickal religion or another, asking them questions about magick and prosperity.

None of these spells represent quick fix-it solutions for your financial security, but each one covers a facet of what you may be experiencing and what to change. If you perform these spells faithfully, coupled with your manifesting work, you should succeed in financial independence. I did.

As you work some of these spells, you may feel yourself fighting against the affirmations, or getting a "touchy-yucky"

---

1. *How to Get Out of Debt, Stay Out of Debt & Live Prosperously* by Jerrold Mundis. Bantam Books, 1988. Page 2.

feeling. This subconscious (or even conscious) response is a result of your negative associations with your expenses. Immediately draw this feeling out and purposefully look at it. Don't push the negative feeling aside without looking at that emotion for what it is—just an emotion. Don't give up. Finish each spell by saying:

My expenses do not obligate me to suffer mentally, physically, or spiritually. So mote it be!

If you are like me, it might be hard at first to realize that your expenses are only a temporary manifestation of your previous actions, and you may mentally and emotionally fight against what you think is the end of the world. For the first three weeks of changing my attitude toward my expenses, I had to say my affirmations many times because my thoughts and actions were a result of my own years of negative programming.

To fight my attitude about banishing my expenses, I began on the dark of the moon by lighting a black candle, and saying:

Great Lord and Lady of the universe, assist me in raising my consciousness and extinguishing my debt. So mote it be!

I envisioned myself becoming more compassionate, less judgmental, and free of debt. Now it's your turn!

Quick Cleansings

Sometimes we need a quick cleansing. For example, this evening I finished paying my bills and, although I was proud that I took care of all my expenses and had some money left over, I still felt emotionally dissatisfied. Time to do a quick cleansing.

- Burn sage, using the smoke to remove negative energies.

- Sprinkle blessed spring water around the house.

- Carry a blessed egg around the house, imagining the negativity entering the egg. Throw the egg away.

Now that you have cleansed and purified your body, mind, and soul, and opened the door for positive energies to come to you, it's time to specifically delve into removing those debts from your life!

Spell for the Desperate

Before we begin methodically working through your debt, you may need a quick spell to get you moving in the right direction. If there is a bill collector at the door or they've just picked you up for bounced checks (hey, it can happen), here's a spell to help you out. I warn you, though, this isn't going to fix the mess you got yourself into—but it will help to relieve the financial pressure until you can get your head on straight.

> **Supplies:** Three green candles; six brown candles; one dish of water; one lodestone (can substitute a magnet); one package of needles; four eggs; crushed mint.

> **Instructions:** Empower the green and brown candles for the monetary amount you desperately need. Carve that amount into each candle with a pin or needle. Set one green candle between two brown candles. (Put the other candles aside to be used for the next two days.) Empower the eggs to draw negativity away from you and your house. Set the lodestone in the dish of water. Sprinkle with crushed mint. Hold your hands over the dish

and ask that the amount of money you specified be drawn to you. Sprinkle the needles into the water (they should attach themselves to the lodestone). Light the candles, saying: "**Debt scatter, money gather.**" Say the amount of money that you need aloud three times. Take the four eggs and place one egg in each of the four corners of your house. Let the candles burn completely. Wait twenty-four hours. Scatter the needles on your front and back walks, asking that prosperity come to your door. (If you are the anal retentive type, you can leave the needles in a metal—not aluminum—can.) Let the eggs sit in the four corners for seven days (do not break them), then remove them from your property. Cleanse the lodestone and put it in a safe place to be used again for other spells. Repeat the candle burning section of this spell for three consecutive days.

Magick Bill Box

You know that you have to pay your bills, but leaving them strewn across the desk where they are a constant reminder of your financial insecurity isn't the best idea in the world. It also isn't good to stuff all your bills in a brown paper bag and shove them in the closet. Although the bills will be out of sight (and possibly out of mind), you may just forget that they are there, which wouldn't be so good for your financial well-being either. I decided to find a positive place to put my bills until I could pay them, remove the negativity from them, and keep me from future overspending—all at the same time.

In this spell we employ the color black (a universal repellent) and a magick mirror empowered to remove negativity. Folktales attribute all sorts of power to mirrors, including the belief that through a mirror, one can see the shadow soul of oneself or another. Mirrors were also thought to deflect or sometimes absorb negativity, and that's how we're going to use them in this spell.

The goddess energy used in this spell is Juno Moneta, the Roman Mother Goddess, who is seen as the guardian of the family and protectress of commerce and travel (the symbol for Juno is on page 148). Coins of precious metals were minted at the temple Capitoline (however, some historical references indicated that the money was minted at the temple of Juno Moneta) so that the money would carry the blessing of the goddess. Her coins were thought to carry the energy of good fortune and healing. Juno is closely connected to the moon, making her association with lunar magick a strong one. Those who worshiped the Roman pantheon believed that every woman had her personal "Juno" whom she honored on her birthday, where every man had his personal "genius." Like many goddesses, Juno had many faces (or facets) to her personality. In honor of Juno Unixia, the woman of the house would anoint the doors, asking for blessings, prosperity, and protection for those who resided within. Juno has two feast days, the first on March 1 in honor of married women and the second on July 7 in respect for her salvation of the Romans during a time of battle. Juno's favorite animal is the goose.

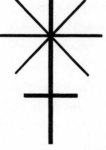

Juno symbol

We're going to use crushed cloves, excellent for the banishment of negativity, protection of your riches, and attraction of new money.

Supplies: One sturdy shoe box (or a colorful box of your
choice); a paint brush; decorative paints, including
plenty of black; one black marker; glue; favorite pictures;
½ ounce crushed cloves; six small mirrors (you can pick
these up at a craft shop for only a few dollars; as a substitute, cut six round pieces of tinfoil); a small piece of gold
or silver (again, you can substitute a small disk of
smooth tinfoil; when I first designed this spell I used the
tinfoil for the mirrors and the small disk, and the spell
worked just fine).

Instructions: Using the black marker, seal the back of each
mirror with an equal-armed cross (page 56). Paint the
inside of the box completely black, including the underside
of the lid. Allow to dry. Glue the six mirrors inside the
box, one on each side. Allow to dry. Empower the inside
of the box to absorb any negativity. Decorate the outside
of the box with your paints and favorite pictures. Glue the
piece of gold or silver on the outside lid of the box.

Take the box to the four quarters (E, S, W, N), beginning with the east, and ask for blessings of prosperity
and the ability to pay what you owe on time without

negative circumstances. Hold your hands over the box, and say:

Gracious Juno, supreme Mother Goddess.
In your name I empower this box to absorb all
negativity associated with my finances and the bills
I place herein. I ask for blessings of future good
fortune and healing, and that every penny I spend
comes back to me threefold, so that all debts will be
resolved quickly. Magick mirrors, consume any
negativity sent to me from another in association
with these bills and return that negativity from
whence it came. With harm to none, so mote it be!

Put your box on your desk, hutch, or kitchen counter—wherever it will be easiest to get to when it is time to pay your bills. As your bills come in, place them in the box until you are ready to pay them. As you put the bill in the box, you can say the following:

Gracious Juno. Supreme Mother.
Please banish any negativity from this bill.

**Bless me with good fortune and healing.
As I will, with harm to none, so mote it be!**

Place the bills in the box. Sprinkle them with crushed cloves, saying:

**Cloves, plant of Jupiter, banish all negativity from
these expenses in this world, and in the world of
phantasm. Bring me reduction of debt and new riches.
With harm to none, so mote it be!**

Close the lid and touch the top, saying:

**Gracious Juno, assist me to build a strong and sturdy
financial future, debt-free, with feelings of security.
With harm to none, so mote it be!**

Sometimes you may be in a hurry, so you could say
"Blessings upon me," as you place the bill in the box.
Be sure to keep the box tightly covered until you are
ready to sit down and pay the bills.

To enhance this spell:

- Add Juno's astrological symbol (page 148) to your box design.

- Make the box during the full moon.

- Pay your bills on Saturday in the hour of Saturn (to banish).

- Give a food offering to Juno, preferably in the woods.

- Add one goose feather to the contents of the box.

- Add a piece of amethyst to the contents of the box to repel negativity.

- Make the box on March 1 or July 7.

The Abracadabra Spell for Diminishing Debts

This spell is great for helping you diminish any old debts you may have incurred, including those standard, monthly debts. In ancient Hebrew the word *abracadabra* means "hurl your thunderbolt even unto death," and it was associated with a thunderbolt deity who perished by throwing himself on the planet so that the creatures of earth could live. Other scholars feel that the Hebrew interpretation of the word should be *ab* (father) *ben* (son) and *ruach acadsch* (holy spirit). There is also debate that the word is Chaldean in origin and not part of cabalistic interpretation at all. Regardless, we know two things: the deity associated with this charm is definitely male in origin, and the word first occurs in the writings of Severus Sammonicus, a Gnostic physician of the second century. We also know that the name became an incantation of its own, used to rid the wearer of sickness or poverty. We are going to do the same thing, and use the charm to eliminate your old debts.

Instruction: As soon as any bill comes in the mail, write the following on the envelope:

Abracadabra
Abracadabr
Abracadab
Abracada
Abracad
Abraca
Abrac
Abra
Abr
Ab
A

Now, turn the bill over and write the full amount you owe; for example:

$995.34
$995.3
$995
$99
$9
$

Put the bill in your Magick Bill Box until you are ready to pay it.

I found that by consciously "doing something" with each bill (even when I didn't have the money to pay the bill), I was mentally and physically reaffirming my power over my finances and banishing my dread. The positive thought that you are working the best way you know how to empower yourself and your finances gives you an edge.

To enhance this spell:

- For a really nasty bill, repeat the spell on a Saturday in the hour of Saturn.

- Roll up the envelope the bill comes in, sprinkle with vinegar, and burn immediately.

When to Pay What Bill

In chapter 3 we talked about money-in and money-out. Few of us have the luxury of paying all of our bills as soon as they come in, although the more you work prosperity magick, the quicker you will obtain the bill-paying schedule that you desire to control your money-out days. Some people like to pay their bills all at once, where others prefer to pay them as they come in. I used to wait until I felt good about paying them—which was unwise because I really didn't want to pay them at all. The idea is to develop the schedule that fits your lifestyle and gets those expenses paid on time. Take a few moments and consider how you want to pay the money you owe. Monthly? Weekly? When the bills come in? Once you have a goal in mind, you are one step closer to financial security.

Most debt schedules give you some leeway in paying what you owe without penalty. There is usually a two- to three-week window from the time you receive a bill to the requested date of payment, which allows you to choose which day to write the check and mail the payment. In most cases we can even rearrange payment schedules with a simple phone call or a nicely written letter. In the upcoming Seven Sisters Spell, we perform our bill-paying routine on Saturday, the magickal day of banishing. Can we pay our bills on other days if we want to? Certainly. Remember, bills aren't the only way we expend money. You might want to send a check to cover a vacation, invest in a favorite stock, or put money in your savings account. Although these activities are considered money-out (since the money is leaving your hands), the ultimate desire can be considered a gain. Let's go over the other six days of the week to determine if you have a bill or two that would be better paid on a different day. Keep in mind that we use the new and waxing moon to pull energies toward us, and the full and waning moons to push things away from us.

Sunday (Planet: Sun). Sunday is considered a day of success. On this day, use your money to obtain a favor, pay for preventative health care, advertise for your business, pay advance vacation expenses, invest in the stock market, and add money to your savings account. Although many establishments are closed on Sundays (especially in small American towns or overseas), you can still mail your payments on Sunday. To make your money pull double duty, mail on a Sunday in the hour of the sun. Empower a bit of gold glitter for financial success and sprinkle the glitter on your envelope. Sunday is a good day to collect money from others. Pay gas, electric, or heating oil bills today.

Monday (Planet: Moon). Monday rules borrowing and lending money as well as family and household affairs. Sign contracts and agreements on a Monday when the moon is waxing. Use Mondays to pay for school supplies, purchase clothing for your children or spouse, invest in repairs, or buy big-ticket items for the home. This is the day to make life and car insurance payments. Monday also covers expenses associated with short trips and public relations, your house payment or apartment rent, as well as taking care of the water bill. Buy groceries today. Borrowing and lending activities fall under the energy of the moon. The moon in the first and second quarter favors the lender, where the moon in the third and fourth quarters favors the borrower. Make purchases for your family garden on this day.

Tuesday (Planet: Mars). Tuesday is the War Day, with aggressive energies. To increase your chances of winning a legal battle, pay associated bills on Tuesday during the waxing moon. If you are being sued, then pay those legal bills on Tuesday on a waning moon.

Expenses related to tools, guns, metals, your health club, surgery, pool membership, sporting equipment, golf lessons, and so on, fall under Mars energy.

Wednesday (Planet: Mercury). Wednesday is the primary day of communication and correspondence. If you need to send correspondence with your payments, mail on Wednesday in the appropriate moon phase. Wednesday covers education, general travel, siblings, neighbors, sales, writing, and computers. Expenses related to your telephone, the Internet, cable, or satellite communications fall under the auspices of Wednesday and Mercury.

Thursday (Planet: Jupiter). Thursday is the Money Day. Focus on investments, new ventures, publishing activities, business expansion, and overseas travel. Payments for college or other educational activities fall here. This is a good day to pay general legal and accounting expenses. If you wish to sell something to pay a particular bill, begin on a Thursday during the waxing moon. Thursday is also the day to buy or sell your car, make car payments, invest in mass transportation tickets, negotiate airline tickets, pay car inspections or repairs, or pay the lease to the parking garage.

Friday (Planet: Venus). The Love Day. Purchase gifts for others, cosmetic products, art, and music items on this day. Buy those season tickets to the opera or sporting events. Things for your living space that are "just for pretty" fall under the energies of Friday and Venus. Fridays are good for hairdresser or barber appointments. If you are involved in planning a wedding, shower, or anniversary bash, Friday is the day for those final payments. Bills involving music or art lessons should be paid on this day.

Saturday (Planet: Saturn). Saturday is the primary banishing day. For anything you want to get rid of, this is the day to pay it off, especially bills relating to final real estate payments, dentists, and situations that have been opposing you.

Seven Sisters Spell to Pay Your Bills

Supplies: A black pen (for banishing debt); one black candle (white will do if you don't have a black one); ⅛ ounce each angelica, cloves, cinnamon; a fireproof bowl; incense of your choice; small metal dish; blessed spring water. Practice drawing a seven-pointed star (the symbol of the seven sisters).

Star of the seven sisters

Instructions: On Saturday, in the hour of Saturn, clear off your kitchen or dining room table. Take your bills from the Magick Bill Box and draw a banishing pentacle in the air over the stack of bills, then set aside any trash—you know, inserts, those special offers that will just cost you more money, and the torn mailing envelopes that already have your Abracadabra Spell written on them.

If you did not write the Abracadabra Spell on the old envelopes, do so now. When you are finished, burn the trash in a small metal dish, envisioning your debts leaving you. Crush the angelica, cloves, and cinnamon together and mix into the ashes (all three herbs have great banishing properties). Throw the ashes to the winds, asking that your debts be banished from your life

with harm to none. (If
you can't do this on a
Saturday, choose a
particularly windy day
or perform during a
great rain storm.)

Banishing pentacle

Light a black candle
(you can use the same
candle each time you pay
your bills, just don't use
this candle for anything
else). Envision the light of this candle banishing your
financial worries. With the candle, draw a banishing pentacle in the air over the stack of bills. Let the candle continue to burn. Pay each bill, saying:

**I banish any negativity associated with these expenses
from my life, whether real or imagined, whether physical or in the world of the unseen. I specifically banish**
(name the bill). **I affirm that my bank account from
which this bill is paid is merely a tool,
not a representation of myself.**

If this is a one-time bill, or the closure of a loan or credit card debt, you can say:

I banish this *(say the name)*
***permanently* from my life.**

As long as you have not signed a contract that penalizes you if you pay back a loan early, add an extra seven dollars on your loan payment. If you are pinched for cash, you can add an extra seventy cents to all other bills. The number seven belongs to the seven sisters, guardians of the *axis mundi* (women of the stars). These seven sisters permeated the mythos structure of almost every great culture, including the Middle East (Seven Pillars of Wisdom); Egypt (Seven Hathors); Arabia (Seven Sages); and Southeast Asia (Seven Mothers of the World). If you prefer to add male deities to this spell, you can use the Seven African Powers (which includes gods and goddesses) or you can invoke the Seven Sages of Greece (men noted for their wisdom).

This bill-paying technique also helps you curb frivolous spending. As your income grows, you won't be as quick to buy that great whatever that you'll never use but lusted after anyway.

Seal the envelope that contains your payment with a mixture of your saliva and blessed spring water, saying:

**In the name of the seven sisters,
doves, mothers, pillars, stars,
I remove these expenses from my life.
May I walk with future wisdom.
With harm to none, so mote it be!**

Draw the symbol of the seven sisters in the corner of the envelope. (If you can't get that star down right, you can simply put the number seven in the lower left-hand corner on the face of the envelope.)

To enhance this spell:

- Perform on October 31 (Samhain) or New Year's Day.

- Perform on a Saturday in the hour of Saturn.

- Perform when the moon is in Capricorn (especially if you have worked hard for your money).

- Perform on the dark of the moon, a full moon, or when the moon is waning.

Magickal Tips When Writing Checks or Money Orders

- Use a black pen to banish debts.

- Seal the check with an equal-armed cross (not a big cross, just a little one in the memo corner) to keep any debt from increasing, and say:

    **My life belongs to me. I live for myself.
    I do not live for those to whom I owe money.**[2]

- If the check is an investment, use a green-inked pen to promote growth.

- For those of you who play the numbers game with negative check balances (meaning you have a habit of writing checks for money that isn't there), ward your checkbook. That's right. Visualize a big hairy monster, a maniacal beast, a growling gargoyle (or whatever) sitting on top of your checkbook.

----

2. *How to Get Out of Debt, Stay Out of Debt & Live Prosperously* by Jerrold Mundis. Bantam Books, 1988. Page 2.

Make sure there is poisonous spittle coming out of its mouth. It will only activate if you are about to do a no-no. Just see how quick you pull your hand away with that visualization!

When You Mail Your Bills

Before you send your bills in the mail, hold them in your hands, and say:

> **I am not the sum total of my monetary debts.**
> **In the name of the Great Mother Juno,**
> **as these bills leave my hands,**
> **I banish negativity and**
> **reduce my financial responsibilities.**
> **So mote it be!**

This spell works especially well if you have done the previous magickal work mentioned in this chapter. Check out the bill-paying correspondence on pages 157–160 and choose the day to mail your bill(s) that matches your intent. You can control money-out days through your bill-paying methods.

Relieving the Debt Monster's Emotional Pressure

A hundred years from now, no one will care what you owe and what you don't (nor will you, for that matter). It isn't necessary to lose sleep, stop eating, or contemplate the fact that you won't owe any money to anyone should you attempt to segue to the other side of life.

The first step in relieving the pressure of debt and curbing those financial woes is to admit that you have a problem and, more importantly, to realize that *any* problem can be solved. Yes, that's right—you have created the dreaded Debt Monster and now you have to disassemble (or is it zap?) it. You may be saying, "But I don't *have* a problem, I just want to make *more* money." That's okay, as long as you aren't in denial. Denial, in this case, is refusing to admit that you've got rough waters in the sea of your personal finances, complete with the dreaded

Debt Monster. And, if you are worried about any current expenses, or finances in general, you have a problem. Admit it and get over it. Sometimes admitting that we have financial difficulties makes us angry, or sad, or even hysterical. That's okay, too. Expect these emotions, process them, and let them go.

For this spell, we are going to call on the good graces of the Sisters of Wyrd, called the Norns—Verdandi, Urd, and Skuld. These three legendary Norse ladies are responsible for weaving the web of your personal fate (the Web of Wyrd). Skuld is the youngest of the Norns and not quite as benevolent as the other two. She is often depicted wearing a veil and carrying a scroll in one hand and a pair of scissors or a knife in the other. Her job is to cut the final strand of your destiny, and her primary element is water. Urd is the mother and guardian of the lot, and thought to be the oldest sister (as her mythos is older than that of Skuld and Verdandi). She focuses on the past. The third sister, Verdandi, represents your present circumstances. She too holds water as her element. While neither the Gods nor humans can order these ladies around or change their collective decree, one can entreat their assistance.

Supplies: One half-full plastic soda bottle (your choice of flavor); one black ribbon, thirteen inches long; one pair of scissors; one permanent black marker; a large bowl.

Sisters of the Wyrd sigil

Instructions: During the dark of the moon, gather your supplies. Envision white light around you. Carry the soda bottle and the ribbon to the four directions (N, E, S, W), and in your own words ask for relief from the stresses of your debts. Draw the sigil for the Sisters of the Wyrd (above) on the bottle with the black marker.

Blow nine times into the plastic soda bottle, after each breath saying:

I surrender my financial worries to Divinity.

After you have blown the ninth breath, cap the bottle.

Now shake up that bottle and, as you do, repeat the same line ("**I surrender my financial worries to Divinity**"). Let all your frustration, unhappiness, and worry work themselves into the fizz of the soda. When you feel ready, stand back and uncap the bottle, allowing the contents to rise and overflow into the bowl. Visualize your monetary stress fizzing away from you. Pour the remainder of the soda into the bowl. Set the soda bottle aside. Hold the black ribbon in your hands, and say:

This ribbon represents the negativity that has attached itself to me and the negative emotions I have experienced over my personal finances. It represents the negative Web of Wyrd attached to my finances. I fully understand that I created these circumstances myself, and now I will extricate myself from them. In the name of the sisters of the Wyrd, I entreat your help in cutting the negativity out of my life. Blessed ladies of the Wyrd, I ask for your gentle assistance in this matter. Urd, mother of the past. Verdandi, sister of the present. Skuld, maiden of

the future and wielder of the sacred scissors.
With harm to none. Gently cut this debt
and negativity from me. So mote it be!

Cut the black ribbon. Burn both pieces. Take the soda
outside, and say:

As I pour this liquid into the ground, I ask for the
blessings of the three sisters to be upon me.
With harm to none, so mote it be!

Practice this spell once a month until you are debt-free.

Don't Spend Today— Breathe Easier Tomorrow

The best way to get out of the spending habit is to stop creating new expenses! Sounds simple, but it isn't always that easy.
You've got to get rather imaginative about it sometimes.
There are expenses you realistically can't get away from—for
example, the light bill, the phone bill, the heating bill, the

water bill . . . shall I continue?—but you can use your noggin without overreacting.

Supplies: A pack of sticky notes or three-by-five-inch cards; cellophane tape.

Instructions: First, you have to determine what is normal usage for you on those monthly bills, like the phone, electricity, water, gas, and so on. If you aren't sure, check around with your friends or family members to find out how much their utilities are costing them. Pick a utility bill out of the pile. Let's use the phone bill. (You've already written your Abracadabra Spell on it, right?) My regular phone bill is thirty-six dollars a month. That includes my caller-ID system. That does not include long-distance calls. The idea of diminishing

utility debts is not to cut yourself off from something that you need, but to find an average dollar amount that you feel comfortable spending. I felt that thirty-six dollars was enough to spend on the phone, so I made a new rule:

"No long-distance phone calls unless it is an emergency or a must-call for business." That's it. That adds an extra five dollars a month to the bill, no more. No call waiting. No call forwarding. No two-party calls. No long-distance calling. At first, people were insulted. Tough. They didn't have to pay my phone bill, I did. After awhile, they got over it.

I wrote my limit on a note and pasted it on my phone. Every time my hand went to the phone to make a long-distance call, I snapped it back and thought twice. That was two years ago. Today my average phone bill is still thirty-six dollars a month (even with the rate increases), I still enjoy my caller-ID service, and the note is no longer necessary. An added benefit is that I've trained my children the same way (although it took my oldest daughter the catastrophe of having her own phone with her first bill at two hundred dollars to figure out why I'd made the restriction on the family phone in the first place)!

Bottom line, you can use this technique on any utility without crippling yourself. I managed to reduce my electric bill by over fifty dollars just by taping little notes on the light switches that said, "Do I really need to be turned on right now?" Hey, be creative! Draw funny little cartoons on your notes. Empower your notes to help you cut down on wasteful habits. It's fun!

Do I Really Need It?

Here's another trick that isn't a spell, but since I'm on the subject, I'll share this one with you, too. It took me several adult years to realize that I had a problem with my finances. One day I realized that if I didn't *do* something, I was going to continue to be miserable. And I was fed up with being miserable. At the time I was about $7,000 in debt (not bad, but not good), and most of it was for back taxes incurred over seven years before. For the last four years I hadn't incurred any new debt (or so I thought) and I was moaning over this old debt that just wouldn't go away. It hung there like an ugly fly, masticating on my life.

I started small (big things make me nervous, you know). I had already instituted my "limit" program, listed above, and then I sat down with all my bills and looked at what I'd been spending my money on. I did not like what I saw. Horror of horrors! I decided to stop taking my kids with me to the grocery store. Yes, I'm weak. They would beg and, most of the time, wanting to be a good, kind parent, I would give in. Since they gave me such a bad time when I left without them, I started going to the grocery store (or any other errand that involved a store) while they were in school. That was great for the spring, fall, and winter, but what about the summer? I scheduled my errands only when I knew other adults would be present. *Voilà!* No buying junk that would break in thirty seconds. In one month I saved over one hundred dollars. The next month I saved two hundred dollars.

Secondly, I looked at each bill and asked, "Do I *really* need this?" I discovered that I didn't have time to read the magazines I had subscriptions to. Cancel. I didn't need that extra cable channel that nobody watched. Cancel. I didn't need a newspaper subscription. Anything I wanted to read about current events, I could get off the Internet. Cancel. I didn't need to belong to the video club. Cancel. I didn't need to belong to the book club. It wasn't saving me money, I was spending more money because of it. Cancel. And so on. Within three months I had those unnecessary bills paid off and cancelled, saving me another one hundred and fifty dollars.

Thirdly, I threw away all junk mail, advertisements, and circulars without opening them. Who needs it? I was tired of being seduced by people I didn't even know. Then, for two weeks, I refused to purchase anything under two dollars (to show myself how much I'd been nickel-and-diming myself).

Spell to Curb Frivolous Spending

This is a very easy spell. Take one lemon and punch a hole with a pencil halfway through the fruit. On a small piece of paper, write: "Please help me curb my frivolous spending habits without harming my prosperity or per-sonal desires." Roll up the paper and put the scroll in the lemon. Tie the lemon with a black ribbon and hang near your kitchen window. After performing this spell, I took my personal campaign even further. I decided to banish my financial fog.

Banishing the Financial Fog

I know some of you are going to groan at this next part. When I was going about cleaning up my financial act, people suggested that I employ a special technique that so frightened me, so distressed me, that I said, "Nothing doing! That's a waste of my time. It will upset me and therefore, I *won't* do it." Six months later, due to the other magickal work I'd been practicing, my finances were recovering, but I realized that if I didn't bite the proverbial bullet, I would never reach my intended goal of financial freedom. So, what am I talking about? What suspenseful, terrible thing am I addressing here?

You are now about to enter the nerve center of your financial success—the list of your expenses. (Oh! Shudder! I knew you would make a face like that.) I didn't particularly care for it either but, like Mary Poppins used to say, "A spoonful of sugar helps the medicine go down." (So drink some soda pop or eat a candy bar, and let's get back to our list.) Besides, I've come up with some fun ideas to keep the process from being too painful.

The first time I tried making this beastly list I used a computer spreadsheet program that only allowed me enough lines for my major expenses. Maybe that was a good thing. I had a general idea what I was responsible for, and the list wasn't that hard to compile, nor did it take me very long to put it together. Whew! That wasn't so bad after all. Later, I discovered that most written material on prosperity insists that you make up a list of every expenditure that you have, down to the thirty cents you lent to Patricia-Sue this morning. That would have been far too daunting a task for me (a Virgo who doesn't usually have a problem making lists) because I still had deeply buried negative emotions attached to my finances that I had not worked through. Eventually I made that dratted list, and since I lived to tell about it—it wasn't *really* all that traumatic.

In the interim, however, I realized that a big chunk of my money remained unaccounted for. According to my list, I should have had plenty of money to pay off my back taxes and do some of the home repairs I'd been thinking about. Where did that money go? Ah, a mystery! I enjoy mysteries (normally).

For the next two months, whenever I bought anything, I asked for a receipt. I know this sounds silly, but it was the

only way I could make the jump from the expenses I knew
I had to the black hole that gobbled up my remaining cash.
To solve the problem I created a . . .

Magickal Receipt Envelope

In this spell, we use the power of the holy serpent. The symbol of the serpent is one of the oldest symbols of power, containing both male and female connotations; it is thought that
the original female oracle of the Delphi Temple—when the
temple was no more than a cave dedicated to the earth goddess Gaia—was called the Pythoness (later called the Pithea).
In India the Goddess of Earth is sometimes called "Serpent
Queen." As the female serpent Kundalini, she represents the
inner power of the human body, coiled in the pelvis. Early
Gnostics worshiped the serpent not as a provider of evil but
as a benevolent feminine aspect of Spirit opposing evil
through truth. The history of the holy snake linked with positive forces and the feminine principle is not easy to find in
standard mythological dictionaries. I guess her truth strikes
too close to home.

In this spell, we use the holy serpent to bring us wisdom, truth, and protection from continued overspending. The dollar sign symbol that we are so familiar with today has roots in snake magick, with the "S" truly representing a snake. I bet you'll never draw another dollar sign again without thinking about the power of snake magick!

Supplies: One large envelope—it can be an accordion one (for those of you who are good at this sort of thing), a plastic envelope with a cute little tie (that's the one I finally picked), or just a plain ordinary envelope (trust me, when you get done with the envelope it won't be plain and ordinary anymore); permanent markers (your choice of colors); incense of your choice; a green candle.

Note: If you are self-employed, you are probably already collecting receipts for tax purposes. Don't forget to use this technique for those receipts as well (just use a different envelope). You'll also have expenses for which you can't get receipts. School lunches come to mind. Be sure to write those types of expenses down on a receipt you already have (to save paper). Copy all receipts you will need for income tax purposes. File the originals in your tax folder and use the copies for magick.

Instructions: As you collect your receipts, draw a dollar
sign on the back of each one, turning the "S" section of
the sigil into a small snake. If you forget to do this, take
a moment before you perform this spell to mark each
receipt. (You can even use a rubber stamp image of a
snake, if you like, and one of my students even used
snake stickers.) On the dark of the moon (but if you get
the urge to begin this some other time,
go for it), bless the envelope
with the four elements. With
your marker, draw a snake on
the envelope. Put any receipts
you have collected so far in
the envelope.

Visualize yourself surrounded by
white light. Present the envelope to the four
quarters (N, E, S, W), asking for blessings in this ritual.
Light the incense. Light the candle. Hold the envelope
out away from you and up at eye level. Call the great
serpent of truth and protection. Using a ritual drum is
helpful, but if you don't have one, you can use the technique of ground drumming (literally drumming on the

ground with your hands). Ask that you have clarity when making any future purchases and request protection for your current financial assets. Thank the holy serpent. Allow the green candle to burn completely. Leave the envelope undisturbed for twenty-four hours, then add your new receipts. You will notice a reduction in the number of receipts that you collect, which means your mystery spending reduces.

Warning: When working with the holy serpent, you can't lie, cheat, steal, or be involved in any type of illegal operation. If you do any of these things, the serpent will turn on you and you'll get bitten.

Beating the Credit Card Scam

You're darned if you do, and you're darned if you don't. Here you are, faithfully working through the process of diminishing your expenses, and you get a response like one of the following:

"I'm sorry, sir, but unless you have a major credit card, or a thousand dollars that we can freeze, we can't rent you a car. Might I explain to you the best way to create a credit history for yourself?" (A rental car agency in Virginia.)

I called ten car rental places in a fifty-mile radius. Not even one of them would rent us a car without that thousand-dollar cash deposit.

"Gee, I'm real sorry about this. We'd love to sell you this car, but you have no credit history. You can't tell me that you've paid cash for everything in the last seven years? Are you sure you're not in the witness protection program or something? Now, here's how you create a good credit history . . ."
(A used car salesman in Pennsylvania—a particularly humiliating experience, if I may add.)

"A room for the night? No major credit card? I'm sorry, but we can't help you. Let me share with you how to create a good credit history so this won't happen to you again . . ."
(The desk clerk at a 57th Street hotel in New York City at midnight.) I had to get pretty pushy with the manager.

"Just give me your credit card number, and we'll put that order through for you. You don't have a credit card? (Slight, breathy pause.) Well then, I suppose you could send us a check . . . let me fill you in on how a credit card would assist you in the future . . ." (An international book order company.)

Argh! My heart still pounds when I think of the humiliation I went through because I insisted on paying cash for over ten years. There I was, being a good customer, and this was how I reaped my reward! Businesses want you to be in debt because that's how they make their money.

To stop the constant embarrassment, I finally got a credit card, but I needed to put some type of restraint on it to keep me from creating more expenses I couldn't handle.

The Ten-Dollar Spell

You can use any monetary denomination you desire for this spell. For purposes of creating good credit history I've used ten dollars, but you could use twenty or even a hundred. You don't have to relegate this spell to financial troubles either. Those of you who are doing just fine can massage the information and make the energies work for your own needs.

Supplies: One ten-dollar bill; a black votive candle; a green candle; your credit cards; spring water; a pinch of cinquefoil; one nail; honey; one piece of tinfoil.

Instructions: Cut the wick off the top of the black candle, flip the candle and dig out the wick (from the bottom end) so you can burn the candle from this opposite end. (This is called "flipping a candle" and the technique is used to reverse negative effects.) Heat the end of the nail and melt a small hole in the new bottom of the black candle. Stuff the hole with cinquefoil. Melt shut. (This is called "loading a candle.") Hold the candle tightly in your hands, and say:

> **Negativity I reverse today.**
> **Bad spending habits go away.**
> **I have food to eat, clothes to wear, and a place to stay.**
> **I know that I will be okay.**
> **With harm to none, so mote it be!**

On a Thursday in the hour of Jupiter, wrap your credit cards once with tin foil, sprinkle with cinquefoil, then wrap again. Cleanse the ten-dollar bill with the four elements to remove any negativity from yourself or previous owners. Place the ten-dollar bill in the center of your magickal working area. Lay the foil packet over the top. Put the black candle on top of the foil packet. Say three times:

**As this candle burns, I diminish my credit card debt
to a running balance of ten dollars
and ten dollars only.**

Then repeat the verse listed in the instructions portion of this spell. Allow the candle to burn completely. Keep your credit cards over the ten-dollar bill as long as possible or until the balance on each card is only ten dollars.

Banishing Blocks to your Financial Success with the Elements

In chapter 2 I showed you how to create abundance with the elements. The next four spells work with the banishing energies of these elements. As with the other spells in this chapter, all four techniques use the phases of the full, waning, or dark of the moon—your choice.

Banishing Blocks with Earth Gnomes

According to the sixteenth-century Swiss alchemist, Paracelsus, the gnome is able to move through earth in the same manner that a fish swims through water or a human walks through air. The word "gnome" may take its meaning from the Greek *ge-nomos*, earth-dweller, and *gnosis*, knowledge. Gnomes are associated with the fey, or fairy-folk, and therefore have distinct personalities and characteristics. Legends vacillate between perceiving them as either friend or foe, but almost all myths equate the gnome to earthly treasures, earth consciousness, and great knowledge of the magick in rocks, caves, roots, gems, and mountains. We find gnomes especially prevalent in German folklore.

Because gnomes can move through earth like fish swim through water, one can turn to the gnomes to move a block of earth energy within oneself, or a block placed in our path by another. I employed the dragon's blood herb for its potency in getting things to move and its ability to protect you while doing so, as well as its herbal association to the earth. This spell is particularly good when things have been moving along just fine for you, you've been recovering from your debts, sailing ahead, and suddenly—thwack! You run into some sort of block. Before you spend months worrying, try this spell.

Supplies: One cup of dirt; a sieve; ½ ounce dragon's blood herb.

Instructions: Over a paper towel or bowl, pour the cup of dirt into the sieve. Add dragon's blood herb. Say:

Element of earth, move the mountain of _____ *(state what is stuck).* **As the dragon's blood mixes with the earth, so shall the blocks in my life be broken gently apart and removed, so that I may prosper.**

As the dirt shakes out of the sieve, visualize the financial problems in your life breaking up and dissolving. Once all the dirt is through the sieve, turn the sieve over and tap it seven times to remove any excess dirt. Carry the dirt to a crossroads at midnight and dump it there, once again asking the element of earth to gently disperse the negativity in your life with harm to none. Wash the sieve, asking the element of water to gently cleanse your situation.

Banishing Blocks with Air Sylphs

The word *sylph* is of Greek derivation, meaning a female spirit of the element of air. This spirit claimed the gift of invisibility. If you listened very hard, you might hear her sweet voice upon the breeze. Greeks considered sylphs akin to angels, showing that belief in angels existed long before Roman Christian conversion. In other cultures, sylphs were thought to be actual ghosts, emanating from the last breath an individual expelled before they died.

During the Christian invasion of Europe, the word *sylph* became a synonym for *Witch*. Charlemagne (768–814 C.E.), who found the Christian wars useful for the spoils and permission of the church for four wives and several concubines, essentially declared that sylphs could not make themselves publicly known. Charlemagne's technique of kill or convert laid the foundation for over five hundred years of sanctified murder, giving the word "sylph" a colorful, if not bloody, history.

Supplies: A small electric fan; thirteen thin yellow ribbons; a black marker. We're using the color yellow as this color is most often associated with the direction of east, the home of the sylphs.

Instructions: On each ribbon, use the black marker to write down your negative feelings about a particular project that is affecting your finances or keeping you from moving ahead with your financial goals. Tie one end of each ribbon securely to the grid that keeps your fingers safe from the whirring blades, allowing the other end of the ribbon to hang free. (Please do this while the fan is turned off and preferably unplugged, just in case.)

Set the fan in front of an open window or open front door. Face the east, open your arms, and invoke the spirits of air, asking that all negativity be banished from your life. If you can, position the fan so that the air can flow through the fan from the east (the place of beginnings) toward the west (the place of transformation). Turn on the fan. Visualize your troubles literally blowing out the window as the ribbons flap in the breeze. Keep the fan on as long as you desire (just be careful that someone doesn't trip over it). If you can, keep the fan running in a denomination of seven (seven minutes, seven hours, or seven days), or run the fan for

seven minutes once a day for seven days. As the blocks
are removed, burn the ribbons, asking that the salamanders dispose of any remaining negativity.

Banishing Blocks with Fire Salamanders

The unique feature about salamanders is that although these
critters are associated with fire, they have the magickal ability to turn fire into ice (and therefore never burn themselves). With this magickal belief, the fate of the poor salamander has never been the same. Live salamanders *do* burn.
Christian mystics and leaders, undaunted by this fact, often
proclaimed the salamander a guardian, with the motto "I
nourish and extinguish."

The properties of fire and ice have a lengthy mythos,
beginning with heathenism and traveling through various
cultures. German-American Witches consider the fire and ice
combination primary over air and earth (although ice isn't
really an element unto itself, as it is frozen water). Regardless
of its mythical associations, fire is not an easy element to
work with for some individuals. I have a student who was

gifted with a fire extinguisher complete with magickal protective sigils. He had a long history of mishaps with the mythical salamanders (not the real ones) and his friends wanted to ensure he would not be consumed in the future. No wonder he prefers working with sylphs!

Supplies: A small outdoor grill that you will use only for magickal work; four red candles (with candleholders); orange, yellow, and red paint. Design and paint five salamanders on the outside of the grill on a Sunday in the hour of Mars or on a Tuesday in the hour of the sun (or any day at midday). Yes, I know, the salamanders will eventually peel off unless you use heat-resistant paint, but that's okay.

Instructions: On a piece of paper, list anything in your life that you feel may contain a block of some sort. You can include health and romance issues, as these categories sometimes intertwine with our financial success. However, the more issues you name, the more changes you will experience. If you think you aren't ready for a passel of new issues, then begin by listing only one or two situations.

On a Tuesday during the waning moon,
envision white light around yourself.
Call the salamanders, asking that they
remove any blocks regarding the issues you
wrote on your paper. Hold the paper
over each unlit candle, repeating the
issues and your desire for an open
pathway. Light each candle,
beginning with the candle that
is closest to the direction of
south. Repeat the issues and
your desire. Hold the paper over the center of the grill
(being careful not to burn yourself). Repeat your desire,
then pass the paper through the flames of the four candles, beginning with the southernmost candle. Drop the
paper in the center of the grill. Watch the paper burn,
whispering until the flame consumes the paper:

**Flame of light, flame of day,
banish blocks in my way.**

Take a deep breath and relax. Scatter the ashes to the
winds, asking the sylphs for assistance. If possible, allow

the candles to burn completely, or use the candles again when you cast the same spell in the future.

Banishing Blocks with Water Undines

Undines are female derivatives of water spirits. Like the other elements, the undines contribute to the universal life force through purification, movement, and sound.

This spell is an old German-American technique using the properties of water turned to ice. Pour spring water into a small, new paper or plastic cup. Freeze.

When you are ready to perform the spell, take the cup out of the freezer. Place upside-down in a bowl. Hold your hands over the ice and name what has frozen in your financial affairs. Blow on the ice three times. Allow the ice to thaw, visualizing the financial difficulty flowing away from you. Chant:

Breath of Spirit,
warmth of love.

To banish a particular bill, write the amount of the bill on a piece of paper and place under the ice.

Collecting Debts

There is nothing more frustrating than to have a person or organization owe you money, especially if they've made no move to pay you back. It's even worse when you owe money, and the amount due you means the difference between having to be in debt again or sailing smoothly toward a debt-free lifestyle.

Concentrate on your emotions first. When someone owes me money and doesn't pay me in the agreed-upon time (or conveniently forgets that they owe me money), I begin to get frustrated. This frustration turns to anger. In the past I didn't say anything because I was taught as a child that it was bad form to create a negative situation. When I finally did say something, I was ridden with guilt. I didn't want to make the person feel bad, I just wanted my money back. I finally realized that I was enabling the situation with my feelings and actions. I was processing the debtor's feelings as my own because I knew what it felt like to owe money. I temporarily solved the problem by making it a policy to never lend money to anyone, which helped me on a personal level until

I could sort my feelings out on the issue. Dealing with major corporations was another matter.

How many times have you called a corporation that owed you money and played the telephone game? Maybell is handling that account and she is at lunch, in a meeting, on a business trip, on vacation in the Bahamas, or has transferred your account to Harry, who is at lunch, in a meeting, on a business trip, or on vacation in the Bahamas (possibly with Maybell). You may also hear: "I'll get back to you tomorrow, on Monday, next Friday, when hell freezes over."

Don't fret. You *do* have options.

- Hire a big man who looks like he is capable of beating the snot out of them.

- Call an attorney and spend more money.

- Camp on their doorstep.

Oh, none of these options practical? Well, let's try some that are.

- Go to the top. That's right. Never fool around with customer service representatives, the secretary, or an assistant. And no, I'm not making fun of these people. I used to *be* these people. I will tell you first-hand that they have no real power to get your money back for you. Their job is to placate you—no more, no less. They can sign you up for new services, correct minor problems, send a service person to your house, and so on, but they do not have the power to cough up your money (no matter how badly they'd like to do just that). So, always find out who runs the show, and go straight to that person.

- Put everything in writing, from the first moment you made contact about the debt. Keep track of who you talked to, when, and what was said.

- Don't be afraid to go after your money.

- Try to collect money on the full or waxing moons. You have a better chance of success.

- Work the You Owe Me Spell.

You ✪we Me Spell

Okay. You've asked nicely, you've gone to the top of the money food chain, and you've put stuff in writing. You are still waiting. Here's a spell to get your money on the move, making its way back to you. Bayberry's primary use in magick is for attraction, whether the issue is love, wishes, or money, and it is sacred to the Greek god Apollo. The marigold lends its energies to fortune and justice smiling upon you (and is especially good for any legal matter).

Supplies: One bayberry candle; bayberry incense; one marigold; an item (or picture) that belongs to the person who owes you (or stationery from the company); a one-dollar bill; one red pen.

Instructions: Write the amount owed to you in red pen on the dollar bill. Wrap the dollar bill around the marigold and the item or picture that represents the individual(s) who owe you money. Place where it won't be disturbed. Ask your guardian angel to assist you in getting your money back. Light the bayberry incense, visualizing the person handing you the money. Light the bayberry candle, continuing the same visualization. Pour seven drops of the bayberry candle wax on top of the dollar bill. Repeat the same visualization. Hold the bill in your hand. Again, repeat the visualization. Finally, repeat the same visualization nightly while holding the dollar bill packet in your hand until you receive your money. After you have received your money, thank Spirit and your guardian angel, undo the packet, donate the dollar bill to a charity, and burn the object that belongs to the individual or company.

Note: This spell will not work if the individual or company does not legitimately owe you money.

To Get a Creditor Off Your Back

The opposite of someone owing you money is for you to owe them money. If someone is harassing you, and you are trying very hard to pay off the debt, try this spell.

Supplies: One lime; a bit of black pepper; a bit of red pepper; seven darning needles; a small piece of paper with the creditor's name written on it.

Instructions: On the full or waning moon, cut a deep equal-armed cross in the lime (do not cut all the way through). Place the paper in the center of the cross as far as you can. Sprinkle with red and black pepper. Close the lime with the darning needles. Ask Spirit to banish the debt and protect you from harassment from the named individual or corporation. Set the lime on the windowsill until the debt is paid.

Don't Give Up

There will be days when you think that all your magickal work has been in vain. Trust me on this one. I've been there. Whatever you do, don't give in or give up. Every little bit you do really *does* count. I had a couple of nasty stretches once I began my plan for success. It does take awhile to bring financial balance into your life and, if you are like me, you'll have a few dips on the way. My husband and I experienced a week or two at different times of the year where all the money had gone out and no money was due to come in for up to seven days. We became resourceful and innovative during those times. In every family atmosphere there will be times of lean and times of fat. How you perform during those times is actually what makes a family strong and independent.

Quickies for Banishing

- List your bills separately on toilet paper and flush the toilet paper down the toilet.

- Open a window to banish negativity.

- Empower a silver spoon and carry it around the house in a counterclockwise direction to banish all negativity. Fill the spoon with sugar and empower to sweeten your opportunities. Leave the spoon undisturbed for seven hours, then cast the sugar to the winds, asking for speedy, positive changes in your life.

- Throw out the old ashes in your fireplace to keep your bills from rising.

- Scatter salt on the windowsills to banish a run of bad luck.

- Place an onion or garlic bulb on the windowsill to collect negativity. Change when the bulb sprouts.

- Once a week, on Saturday, take out all the money in your purse, wallet, and pockets. Cleanse and consecrate the money with the four elements.

- To rid yourself of an unjust bill, knot nine black feathers into a strip of black rawhide or yarn. Wrap a copy of the bill around it. Fold three times. Bury off your property.

- Whenever you change your clothes, visualize poverty leaving you. Conversely, as you dress, visualize positive abundance coming toward you.

- Add a little angelica to your laundry water to banish poverty from your family.

- If you are a golfer, you will love this one (my husband practices this): as you hit the balls on the driving range, visualize poverty sailing across the green and out of your life.

- If someone is threatening you for money you do not owe, or is being unreasonable about your payment (this does happen), write that person's name on an envelope. In the envelope sprinkle nettle, red pepper, black pep-

per, garden nightshade, and graveyard dirt (you can substitute patchouli for the graveyard dirt). Seal. Bury off
your property or burn in an outdoor fire.

- Cross two large needles under your front doormat to
  keep bill collectors away.

General Emergencies

My husband and I worked very hard to find balance in our
financial affairs. As I worked on the prosperity end, he
worked on the savings end—and he did beautifully. By the
time I had our debts resolved, he'd saved over one thousand
dollars. Then a slew of emergencies hit us, dissolving that money like cotton candy in a summer thunderstorm. These are the
toughest times in prosperity magick—
when you think that the balance you
worked so hard for has slipped through
your fingers and you're left staring at
the black hole that birthed the broken
oven element, the new brake system

for your kid's car, the dental bill for your husband's infected tooth, the increase in your trash collection bill, and the deceased vacuum cleaner. *Do not give up.* Emergencies are a part of survival. Panic is *not* an option. Here is a plan of action for emergencies.

- Do a banishing spell to remove any negativity. It doesn't matter what phase the moon is in or what day it is—an emergency is an emergency.

- Continue any regular abundance or banishing work.

- Don't give up and don't give in.

- Coat the bottom of a red candle with honey. Roll in gold glitter. Burn to break any blocks in your life and heat up sluggish energy. Use the candle to focus on pulling general prosperity to you. If it's really bad, carve the symbol for Mars (♂) on your candle.

- Coat the bottom of a purple candle with honey. Roll in silver glitter. Burn to focus on a specific dollar amount to cover the emergency expense.

- Take at least one ritual bath or shower to cleanse your body of any negativity, using ½ cup of lemon juice.

- Purify your house by burning sage every day until the emergency has been resolved. (This is my husband's favorite.)

Epilogue

Sometimes the hardest part of doing a spell is choosing which spell to do and what correspondences should be included. When someone looks through a spellbook to find a particular spell, they often check the name of the spell to see if that name fits their circumstances. If none of the names apply, or if the name isn't specific to the problem, they may feel that the spell isn't the right one. This isn't necessarily the case. Here are a few helpful tips:

- Pick the description that most closely matches your need.

- Check the moon phase to determine whether you should concentrate on banishing or manifesting. Remember, regardless of the moon phase, you can always banish on a Saturday and you can manifest on the other days by using the magick of the day and an appropriate planetary hour if you have an emergency.

Add this rider to your spell: **"May all astrological correspondences be correct for this working."** (Originally written by Laurie Cabot.)

- You can massage the wording of *any* spell to match your needs.

- You don't need tons of stuff to cast a spell. If you can't find an ingredient, then substitute something that closely matches the original ingredient. Keep Scott Cunningham's *Encyclopedia of Magickal Herbs* (Llewellyn, 1992) on hand for herbal substitutions.

- Don't be afraid to do research.

- If you are worried about the results of a spell, you can add the rider: **"May this spell not reverse, or place upon me any curse."** (Originally written by Sybil Leek.)

There isn't a day that goes by where I don't think of you, the reader. With every word I write, every seminar I do, every ritual I perform, I always think about how you are doing and hope that my work continues to assist you on your spiritual path. Although this book is small, I think we covered a lot of positive magickal ground. Remember to work both manifesting and banishing magick when performing magick for your overall prosperity. Once you get your finances straightened out and are experiencing abundance, keep working to enhance your lifestyle. Don't stop because everything's okay now. Just keep going!

To stay updated on my future projects, please check out my web site at **http://www.silverravenwolf.com.** You'll find great information there on my touring schedule, books, and lots of other goodies. I even have two teen pages! I update the web site about once a month, adding new spells and rituals, as well as other information.

Much love and luck to you in your future endeavors!

Silver Raven Wolf

Appendices

Appendix 1: Color Magick Correspondences

Use the lists below when in doubt, but don't view this information as the last word on color magick.

Color Magick Correspondence List

Color	Purpose
Black	Returning to sender; divination; negative work; protection
Blue-Black	For wounded pride; broken bones; angelic protection
Dark Purple	Used for calling up the power of the ancient ones; sigils/runes; government
Lavender	To invoke righteous spirit within yourself and favors for people
Dark Green	Invoking the goddess of regeneration; agriculture; financial
Mint Green	Financial gains (used with gold and silver)
Green	Healing or health; north cardinal point
Avocado Green	Beginnings
Light Green	Improve the weather

Color	Purpose
Indigo Blue	To reveal deep secrets; protection on the astral levels; defenses
Dark Blue	To create confusion (must be used with white or you will confuse yourself)
Blue	Protection
Royal Blue	Power and protection
Pale/Light Blue	Protection of home; buildings; young; young males
Ruby Red	Love or anger of a passionate nature
Red	Love; romantic atmosphere; energy; south cardinal point
Light Red	Deep affection of a non-sexual nature
Deep Pink	Harmony and friendship in the home
Pink	Harmony and friendship with people; binding magick
Pale Pink	Friendship; young females
Yellow	Healing; can also represent east cardinal point
Deep Gold	Prosperity; sun magick
Gold	Attraction
Pale Gold	Prosperity in health
Burnt Orange	Opportunity
Orange	Material gain; to seal a spell; attraction
Dark Brown	Invoking earth for benefits
Brown	Peace in the home; herb magick; friendship
Pale Brown	Material benefits in the home
Silver	Quick money; gambling; invocation of the moon; moon magick

Color	Purpose
Off-White	Peace of mind
Lily White	Mother Candle (burned for thirty minutes at each moon phase)
White	Righteousness; purity, used for east cardinal point; devotional magick
Grey	Glamouries

Use White to substitute for any color.

Colors for Days of the Week

Day	Color
Monday	White
Tuesday	Red
Wednesday	Purple
Thursday	Green
Friday	Blue
Saturday	Black
Sunday	Yellow

Appendix 2: Astrological Symbols

Use for carving on candles.

ZODIAC NAME	GLYPH	MEANING
Aries	♈	To begin a project
Taurus	♉	To gain and keep luxury
Gemini	♊	To create communicative change
Cancer	♋	To work on positive emotions
Leo	♌	To guard what you have
Virgo	♍	To remember the details
Libra	♎	To bring fairness
Scorpio	♏	To intensify anything
Sagittarius	♐	To bring humor and friends
Capricorn	♑	To plan business finances
Aquarius	♒	To bring change and freedom
Pisces	♓	To connect to the spiritual world

PLANETS AND THEIR MEANINGS

Sun = Success

Moon = Family

Venus = Love and fast cash

Mars = To activate anything

Mercury = Communication

Jupiter = Expansion

Saturn = Banish or restrict

Appendix 3: The Planetary Hours[1]

The selection of an auspicious time for beginning a magickal working is an important matter. When a thing is begun, its existence takes on the nature of the conditions under which it was begun.

Each hour of the day is ruled by a planet, and takes on the attributes of that planet. You will notice that planetary hours do not take into account Uranus, Neptune, and Pluto, as they are considered here as higher octaves of Mercury, Venus, and Mars, respectively. For example, if something is ruled by Uranus, you can use the hour of Mercury.

The only other factor you need to know to use the planetary hours is the time of your local sunrise and sunset for any given day, available from your local newspaper. Note: Your sunrise and sunset time may vary from the example if you live in a different location. Your latitude/longitude are already figured into your local paper's sunrise and sunset times.

Step One. Find the sunrise and sunset times for your location for your chosen day from your local paper. We will use January 2, 1999, 10 degrees latitude, as an example. Sunrise for January 2, 1999, at 10 degrees latitude is at 6 hours and 16 minutes (or 6:16 A.M.) and sunset is at 17 hours and 49 minutes (or 5:49 P.M.).

Step Two. Subtract sunrise time (6 hours 16 minutes) from sunset time (17 hours 49 minutes) to get the number of astrological daylight hours. It is easier to do this if you convert the hours into minutes. For example, 6 hours and 16 minutes equals 376 minutes. 17 hours and 49 minutes equals 1,069 minutes. Now subtract: 1,069 minutes minus 376 minutes equals 693 minutes.

----

1. Planetary hour information is condensed from *Llewellyn's 2000 Daily Planetary Guide*, pp. 184–185.

Step Three. Next you should determine how many minutes are in a daylight planetary hour for that particular day. To do this, divide 693 minutes (the number of daylight minutes) by 12. The answer is 58, rounded off. Therefore, a daylight planetary hour for January 2, 1999, at 10 degrees latitude has 58 minutes.

Step Four. Now you know that each daylight planetary hour is roughly 58 minutes. You also know, from step one, that sunrise is at 6:16 A.M. To determine the starting times of each planetary hour, simply add 58 minutes to the sunrise time for the first planetary hour, 58 minutes to that number for the second planetary hour, etc. Therefore, the first hour in our example is 6:16 A.M.–7:14 A.M. The second hour is 7:14 A.M.–8:12 A.M.; and so on. Note that because you rounded up the number of minutes in a sunrise hour, that the last hour doesn't end exactly at sunset. This is a good reason to give yourself a little "fudge space" when using planetary hours. (You could also skip the rounding-up step.)

Step Five. Now, to determine which sign rules which daylight planetary hour, consult your calendar to determine which day of the week January 2 falls on. You'll find it's a Saturday in 1999. Next, turn to page 217 to find the sunrise planetary hour chart. If you follow down the column for Saturday, you will see that the first hour is ruled by Saturn, the second by Jupiter, the third by Mars, and so on.

Step Six. Now you've determined the daytime (sunrise) planetary hours. You can use the same formula to determine the night-time (sunset) planetary hours, using sunset as your beginning time and sunrise the next day as your end time. When you get to step 5, remember to consult the sunset table on page 218 rather than the sunrise one.

Planetary Hours
Sunrise

Hour	Sunday	Monday	Tuesday	Wednesday	Thursday	Friday	Saturday
1	Sun	Moon	Mars	Mercury	Jupiter	Venus	Saturn
2	Venus	Saturn	Sun	Moon	Mars	Mercury	Jupiter
3	Mercury	Jupiter	Venus	Saturn	Sun	Moon	Mars
4	Moon	Mars	Mercury	Jupiter	Venus	Saturn	Sun
5	Saturn	Sun	Moon	Mars	Mercury	Jupiter	Venus
6	Jupiter	Venus	Saturn	Sun	Moon	Mars	Mercury
7	Mars	Mercury	Jupiter	Venus	Saturn	Sun	Moon
8	Sun	Moon	Mars	Mercury	Jupiter	Venus	Saturn
9	Venus	Saturn	Sun	Moon	Mars	Mercury	Jupiter
10	Mercury	Jupiter	Venus	Saturn	Sun	Moon	Mars
11	Moon	Mars	Mercury	Jupiter	Venus	Saturn	Sun
12	Saturn	Sun	Moon	Mars	Mercury	Jupiter	Venus

Planetary Hours
Sunset

Hour	Sunday	Monday	Tuesday	Wednesday	Thursday	Friday	Saturday
1	Jupiter	Venus	Saturn	Sun	Moon	Mars	Mercury
2	Mars	Mercury	Jupiter	Venus	Saturn	Sun	Moon
3	Sun	Moon	Mars	Mercury	Jupiter	Venus	Saturn
4	Venus	Saturn	Sun	Moon	Mars	Mercury	Jupiter
5	Mercury	Jupiter	Venus	Saturn	Sun	Moon	Mars
6	Moon	Mars	Mercury	Jupiter	Venus	Saturn	Sun
7	Saturn	Sun	Moon	Mars	Mercury	Jupiter	Venus
8	Jupiter	Venus	Saturn	Sun	Moon	Mars	Mercury
9	Mars	Mercury	Jupiter	Venus	Saturn	Sun	Moon
10	Sun	Moon	Mars	Mercury	Jupiter	Venus	Saturn
11	Venus	Saturn	Sun	Moon	Mars	Mercury	Jupiter
12	Mercury	Jupiter	Venus	Saturn	Sun	Moon	Mars

Appendix 4: Moon Phases

New Moon

- Moon is 0–45 degrees directly ahead of the sun
- Moon rises at dawn, sets at sunset; for full use of these energies, stick between this time period
- Moon is from exact new moon to 3½ days after
- Purpose: Beginnings
- Workings for: Beauty, health, self-improvement, farms and gardens, job hunting, love and romance, networking, creative ventures
- Pagan Holiday: Winter Solstice (December 22)[2]
- Goddess Name: Rosemerta's Moon
- Goddess Energy: Goddesses of Growth
- Offering: Milk and honey
- Theme: Abundance
- Rune: Feoh for abundance; Cen for openings; Gyfu for love
- Tarot Trump: The Fool

---

2. Due to astrological timing, solstices and equinoxes will not always be on the same date. Other pagan holidays will differ depending on the tradition practiced.

Crescent

- Moon is 45–90 degrees ahead of the sun
- Moon rises at mid-morning, sets after sunset; for full use of these energies, stick between this time period
- Moon is from 3½ to 7 days after the new moon
- Purpose: The movement of the thing
- Workings: Animals, business, change, emotions, matriarchal strength
- Pagan Holiday: Imbolc (February 2)
- Goddess Name: Brigid's Moon
- Goddess Energy: Water Goddesses
- Offering: Candles
- Theme: Manifestation
- Rune: Birca for Beginnings; Ing for focus
- Tarot Trump: The Magician

First Quarter

- Moon is 90–135 degrees ahead of the sun
- Moon rises at noon, sets at midnight; for full use of these energies, stick between this time period
- Moon is from 7 to 10½ days after the new moon
- Purpose: The shape of the thing
- Workings: Courage, elemental magick, friends, luck, and motivation

- Pagan Holiday: Spring Equinox (March 21)
- Goddess Name: Persephone's Moon
- Goddess Energy: Air Goddesses
- Offering: Feathers
- Theme: Luck
- Rune: Algiz for luck; Jera for improvement; Ur for strength
- Tarot Card: Strength or The Star

Gibbous

- Moon is 135–180 degrees ahead of the sun
- Moon rises in mid-afternoon, sets around 3 A.M.; for full use of these energies, stick between this time period
- Moon is between 10½ to 14 days after the new moon
- Purpose: Details
- Workings: Courage, patience, peace, harmony
- Pagan Holiday: Beltaine (May 1)
- Goddess Name: Nuit's Moon
- Goddess Energy: Star Goddesses
- Offering: Ribbons
- Theme: Perfection
- Rune: Asa for eloquence; Wyn for success; Dag for enlightenment
- Tarot Trump: The World

Full Moon

- Moon is 180–225 degrees ahead of the sun
- Moon rises at sunset, sets at dawn; for full use of these energies, stick between this time period
- Moon is from 14 to 17½ days after the new moon
- Purpose: Completion of a project
- Workings: Artistic endeavors, beauty, health, fitness, change, decisions, children, competition, dreams, families, health, knowledge, legal undertakings, love, romance, money, motivation, protection, psychic power, self-improvement
- Pagan Holiday: Summer Solstice (June 21)
- Goddess Name: Sekhmet's Moon
- Goddess Energy: Fire Goddesses
- Offering: Flowers
- Theme: Power
- Rune: Sol
- Tarot Card: The Sun

Disseminating

- Moon is 225–270 degrees ahead of the sun
- Moon rises at mid-evening, sets at mid-morning; for full use of these energies, stick between this time frame
- Moon is 3½ to 7 days after the moon

- Purpose: Initial destruction
- Working: Addiction, decisions, divorce, emotions, stress, protection
- Pagan Holiday: Lammas (August 1)
- Goddess Name: Hecate's Moon
- Goddess Energy: Earth Goddesses
- Offering: Grain or rice
- Theme: Reassessment
- Rune: Thorn for destruction; Algiz for protection; Thorn for defense
- Tarot Trump: The Tower for destruction; Hope for protection

Last Quarter

- Moon is 270–315 degrees ahead of the sun
- Moon rises at midnight and sets at noon; for full use of these energies, stick between this time frame.
- Moon is 7 to 10½ days after the full moon
- Purpose: Absolute destruction
- Working: Addictions, divorce, endings, health and healing (banishing), stress, protection, ancestors
- Pagan Holiday: Fall Equinox (September 21)
- Goddess Name: The Morrigan's Moon
- Goddess Energy: Harvest Goddesses

- Offering: Incense
- Theme: Banishing
- Rune: Hagal; Ken for banishing; Nyd for turning; Isa for binding
- Tarot Trump: Judgement

Balsamic (Dark Moon)

- Moon is 315–360 degrees ahead of the sun
- Moon rises at 3 A.M., sets mid-afternoon; for full use of these energies, stick between this time frame
- Moon is 10½ to 14 days after the full moon
- Purpose: Rest
- Working: Addictions, change, divorce, enemies, justice, obstacles, quarrels, removal, separation, stopping stalkers and theft
- Pagan Holiday: Samhain (October 31)
- Goddess Name: Kali's Moon
- Goddess Energy: Dark Goddesses
- Offering: Honesty
- Theme: Justice
- Rune: Tyr for justice; Ken for banishing
- Tarot Trump: Justice

Bibliography

Biographical Dictionary. New York: Oxford University Press, 1993.

Beyerl, Paul. *A Compendium of Herbal Magick.* Custer, Wash: Phoenix Publishing, Inc., 1998.

Bunson, Matthew. *Angels A to Z—A Who's Who of the Heavenly Host.* New York: Crown Trade Paperbacks, 1996.

Carlson, Richard. *Don't Worry, Make Money.* Hyperion, 1997.

Cunningham, Scott. *Cunningham's Encyclopedia of Magical Herbs.* St. Paul, Minn.: Llewellyn, 1992.

Cunningham, Scott and David Harrington. *The Magical Household.* St. Paul, Minn.: Llewellyn, 1983.

Dixon-Kennedy, Mike. *Celtic Myth & Legend, An A-Z of People and Places.* London, England: Blandford Publishing, 1996.

Graves, Robert. *The White Goddess.* New York: Farrar, Straus and Giroux, 1948, 1986.

Gonzalez-Wippler, Migene. *Rituals and Spells of Santeria.* Plainview, NY: Original Publications, 1984.

———. *Santeria: African Magic in Latin America.* Plainview, NY: Original Publications, 1987.

Jones, Allison. *Larousse Dictionary of World Folklore.* Edinbourough, England: Larousse, 1995.

Leach, Maria, ed. *Funk & Wagnall's Standard Dictionary of Folklore, Mythology, and Legend.* San Francisco: Harper SanFrancisco, 1972.

Lippman, Deborah and Paul Colin. *How to Make Amulets, Charms & Talismans: What They Mean and How to Use Them.* Philadelphia: J. B. Lippincott Company, 1979.

Mercatante, Anthony S. *Facts on File Encyclopedia of World Mythology and Legend.* New York: Oxford, 1988.

Mundis, Jerrold. *How to Get Out of Debt, Stay Out of Debt & Live Prosperously.* New York: Bantam, 1988.

Redmond, Layne. *When the Drummers Were Women.* New York: Three Rivers Press, 1997.

Roman, Sanaya and Duane Packer. *Creating Money: Keys to Abundance.* H. J. Kramer, Inc., 1987.

Stokes, Gillian. *Becoming Prosperous: A Beginner's Guide.* England: Hodder & Stoughton, 1997.

Valiente, Doreen. *An ABC of Witchcraft.* Custer, Wash.: Phoenix, 1973.

Walker, Barbara. *The Woman's Dictionary of Symbols and Sacred Objects.* San Francisco: Harper Collins, 1988.

———. *The Woman's Encyclopedia of Myths and Secrets.* San Francisco: Harper SanFrancisco, 1983.

Index